Samuel French Acting Edition

MW00791144

King of the Yees

by Lauren Yee

SAMUELFRENCH.COM   SAMUELFRENCH.CO.UK

MUSIC USE NOTE

Licensees are solely responsible for obtaining formal written permission from copyright owners to use copyrighted music in the performance of this play and are strongly cautioned to do so. If no such permission is obtained by the licensee, then the licensee must use only original music that the licensee owns and controls. Licensees are solely responsible and liable for all music clearances and shall indemnify the copyright owners of the play(s) and their licensing agent, Samuel French, against any costs, expenses, losses and liabilities arising from the use of music by licensees. Please contact the appropriate music licensing authority in your territory for the rights to any incidental music.

IMPORTANT BILLING AND CREDIT REQUIREMENTS

If you have obtained performance rights to this title, please refer to your licensing agreement for important billing and credit requirements.

KING OF THE YEES had a workshop at the Goodman Theatre in Chicago in 2015. The workshop was directed by Joshua Kahan Brody, with sets by Kevin DePinnet, costumes by Christine Pascual, lighting by Jesse Klug, and sound by Mikhail Fischel. The stage manager was Kim Osgood. The cast was as follows:

LARRY . . . . Francis Jue
LAUREN . . . . Melissa Canciller
ACTOR 1 . . . . .Daniel Smith
ACTOR 2 . . . . Deanna Myers
ACTOR 3 . . . . .Rammel Chan

The world premiere of *KING OF THE YEES* was produced in 2017 by Goodman Theatre, Chicago, Illinois (Robert Falls, Artistic Director; Roche Schulfer, Executive Director) and Center Theatre Group, Los Angeles, California (Michael Ritchie, Artistic Director; Stephen Rountree, Executive Director). The production was directed by Joshua Kahan Brody, with scenic design by William Boles, costume design by Izumi Inaba, lighting design by Heather Gilbert, sound design by Mikhail Fiksel, projection design by Mike Tutaj, dramaturgy by Tanya Palmer, lion dance consultation by LC Liao, assistant direction by Egla Kishta and Sam Roberson, and fight choreography by Chuck Coyl. The stage managers were Donald Claxon and David Franklin. The cast was as follows:

LARRY . . . . Francis Jue
LAUREN . . . . .Stephenie Soohyun Park
ACTOR 1 . . . . .Daniel Smith
ACTOR 2 . . . . .Angela Lin
ACTOR 3 . . . . .Rammel Chan

KING OF THE YEES was commissioned by the Goodman Theatre, with support from the Virginia B. Toulmin Foundation.

CHARACTERS

LARRY– Asian American, male, 60.

LAUREN – Asian American, female, 30.

ACTOR 1 – Asian American, male, 30s–50s. Also plays Someone, the Erhu Player, Parke Skelton, Shrimp Boy, a Lum Elder, and Sichuan Face Changer.

ACTOR 2 – Asian American, female, 20s–40s. Also plays Jenny Pang, the First Lion Dance, Betty Yee, the FBI Agent, a Lum Elder, and the Whiskey Seller.

ACTOR 3 – Asian American, male, 20s–30s. Also plays Danny Ma, Leland Yee, the Chiropractor, a Lum Elder, the Second Lion Dance, and the Model Ancestor.

SETTING

San Francisco, Chinatown

AUTHOR'S NOTES

A lot of this is true. But a lot of it is only kind of true.
Just like the stories your father once told you as a child.

Notes about the play and text

The play runs two hours, including an intermission. The Chinese spoken is Cantonese, a dialect of Southern China.

[Any text in brackets] should be filled in with actual information.

("Any text in parenthesis and quotation marks") is never said. It's just to imply tone.

If there is a slash / in the dialogue, the next actor's line starts at the slash.

Note on projections

Licensees are required to use projections and should create their own where called for in the script.

Special thanks

Paul Yee, Venna Chan, and family (Chicago); Kenny Yee, Donald Yee, Alan Yu (Los Angeles); Kevin Lee, Fred Yee (Seattle); Frank Yee (New York); Henry Yee (Cleveland); David Yee and family, Cheak Yee (Phoenix); Jim Yee, Martin Yee (Vancouver); Anita Luk, Hedgebrook, and Tanya Palmer.

For Zadie Yee Zwillinger.

ACT ONE

The Yee Fung Toy Family Association, Fourth Floor
San Francisco

(In the center of the room is a pair of imposing red double doors. The doors stand alone, unconnected to any wall, like a pair of doors you might find in a museum exhibit.)

*(**ACTOR 2** as "Lauren" speaks to the audience.)*

ACTOR 2 (LAUREN). In San Francisco Chinatown, there is a door on Waverly Place
Wedged between Stockton and Grant, Clay and Sacramento,
A door you have passed by dozens of times.
And on the door is a sign.

> *(**ACTOR 1** appears as "Larry." He has a noticeable Chinese accent.)*

ACTOR 1 (LARRY). *Yee fûng toy goông saw.**

ACTOR 2 (LAUREN). Or –

ACTOR 1 (LARRY). The Yee Fung Toy Family Association!

> *(Gong.)*

ACTOR 2 (LAUREN). And if you want to pass through that door, there is one man in Chinatown who can take you through: my father –

ACTOR 1 (LARRY). Larry. Larry Yee.

ACTOR 2 (LAUREN). "King of the Yees."
Because this is his club.

---

*Yee Fung Toy Family Association

His life.

The thing he cannot let go of.

ACTOR 1 (LARRY). And welcome to the Yee Fung Toy Family Association!

ACTOR 2 (LAUREN). The Yee Fung Toy began nearly a hundred fifty years ago when Chinese workers migrated to America during the Gold Rush and the building of the transcontinental railroad. Barred from bringing their wives and children, the men formed clubs based on last names like –

ACTOR 1 (LARRY). Wong, Lum, Ma.

ACTOR 2 (LAUREN). But most importantly –

ACTOR 1 (LARRY). Yee!

ACTOR 2 (LAUREN). Yet, today, the Yee Fung Toy has become an obsolescent organization. All business is conducted in Cantonese and its aging membership remains almost exclusively male. My father tries to put on a brave face, but sometimes he wonders –

(**ACTOR 1** *as "Larry" seems to hear a noise.*)

ACTOR 1 (LARRY). Anyone there?

ACTOR 2 (LAUREN). And lately, the answer has been no.

ACTOR 1 (LARRY). Well, next time!

ACTOR 2 (LAUREN). This is my dad.

ACTOR 1 (LARRY). That's right!

ACTOR 2 (LAUREN). And this is what he does.

ACTOR 1 (LARRY). Every week!

ACTOR 2 (LAUREN). For nearly twenty years, it has swallowed his life.

ACTOR 1 (LARRY). You gotta support your community!

ACTOR 2 (LAUREN). So he says.

ACTOR 1 (LARRY). You gotta have your own people!

ACTOR 2 (LAUREN). So he thinks.

ACTOR 1 (LARRY). So I know!

ACTOR 2 (LAUREN). I am Lauren Yee and this is a story.

A true story.

About my dad

About dying Chinatowns

About how things fall apart and how to say goodbye.

ACTOR 1 (LARRY). *(Finally hears.)* Goodbye?

ACTOR 2 (LAUREN). Goodbye.

ACTOR 1 (LARRY). Oh, it's uh – *"joy-geen."** That would be the Cantonese. The Mandarin would be, uh – hold on, lemme look it up –

> *(He looks on his phone.)*

Hold on.

ACTOR 2 (LAUREN). He always thinks he has more time.

> *(The real **LARRY** enters – on the phone, holding a cardboard box – as quietly as he can, which is actually very loudly. **LAUREN** clocks his entrance.)*

LARRY. *(Phone.)* Dee, I can't talk right now. I'm in Lauren's play. Lauren's play!

ACTOR 2 (LAUREN). But deep down he must know / that –

LARRY. *(Phone.)* How is it? Eh, you know.

ACTOR 2 (LAUREN). But deep down / he must know that his way of life –

> *(Crash.)*

LAUREN. Hold please!

> *(Lights go up. **LARRY** is sprawled on the floor, the contents of his box strewn on the stage.)*

Daddy!

LARRY. Ohp, sorry! Sorry.

LAUREN. Are you okay?!

LARRY. I'm okay, I'm just – *(Tests out his ankle.)* Oh shoot, think I popped my ankle.

ACTOR 1. Here, take a seat.

ACTOR 2. We'll get that.

---

*goodbye

LARRY. Ohp. Ohp.

> (**ACTORS 1** *and* **2** *help* **LARRY** *up, put the things back in his box.*)

LAUREN. Maybe you can sit over / there.

> (**LARRY** *sits down heavily right in the middle of the stage.*)

LARRY. Ahhhh.

(To audience.) I'm Larry. Larry Yee.

ACTOR 1. You're the Larry?

LARRY. That's the me!

(To audience.) And Imma part of the Yee Fung Toy Family Association. Which is this building we are in right now.

LAUREN. They know that.

LARRY. But you tell 'em how the Yees got branches all over the country?

LAUREN. Uh-huh.

ACTOR 1. Actually, I don't know if you've mentioned that.

ACTOR 2. Yeah.

LAUREN. Oh. Well.

(To audience.) The Yee Fung Toy –

LARRY. Yee Fung Toy.

> *(The difference is really, really small.)*

LAUREN. Yee Fung Toy.

LARRY. Fung Toy.

LAUREN. Fung Toy.

LARRY. Fung Toy.

ACTOR 2. Fung Toy.

LARRY. There you go!

LAUREN. The Yees have branches all over the country!

LARRY. Not as big as the Wongs, but we're pretty up there. We got four floors in this building 'cause San Francisco's the headquarters. This room here's where we hold the board meetings. Normally, we don't let non-Yees come in here, but we let her use it 'cause she's my daughter.

LAUREN. Thank you, Daddy.

LARRY. Lauren. Lauren Yee.

LAUREN. I introduced myself –

LARRY. You did?

LAUREN. When we started.

LARRY. You started?

LAUREN. Yeah.

LARRY. *(To audience.)* I apologize. I was late.

LAUREN. That's okay. You weren't even invited.

LARRY. *(To audience.)* Sorry, I don't know the rules. I'm just a telephone man. My daughter she's the playwright! Moved all the way out to New York! East Coast! Nobody knows why!

LAUREN. That's not true.

LARRY. Nobody knows!

LAUREN. I went to college.

LARRY. Yale!

LAUREN. I met my husband. I got married.

LARRY. She's been married for two years…and nine months.

LAUREN. No, I haven't.

LARRY. *(To audience, nods.)* And nine months. Her husband Zach. Jewish! He's a lawyer out in New York.

ACTOR 1. Wait, but aren't you moving?

LAUREN. No?

ACTOR 1. To Germany.

ACTOR 2. Oh that's right!

LARRY. What?!

ACTOR 2. You were mentioning.

LARRY. She already lives in New York. Why'd she be moving to Germany?

LAUREN. For Zach's job…maybe.

LARRY. Germany?

LAUREN. Yeah.

LARRY. *(To audience.)* My daughter so full of surprises.

LAUREN. Mm-hm. Let's get back to the play.

LARRY. *(Re: ACTORS.)* So this's the play, huh?

LAUREN. Yep.

LARRY. So small.

LAUREN. It's a two-hander.

LARRY. *(To ACTORS 1 and 2.)* So how's it going, uh – I didn't catch your names.

LAUREN. This is [first name of Actor 2] and that's [first name of Actor 1].

(**ACTORS 1** and **2** *wave.*)

ACTOR 1. I play you!

LARRY. Me?!

ACTOR 2. He's really good.

ACTOR 1. Wellll.

LARRY. I'm in the play?

ACTOR 1. Uh-huh.

LAUREN. For like two seconds.

LARRY. *(Relieved.)* Oh, like a extra.

LAUREN. Yes, like an extra.

ACTOR 1. Not that much of an extra.

LARRY. Looks just like me!

(**ACTOR 1** *doesn't look like* **LARRY** *at all.*)

(To audience.) Which is me? Which is him? No idea!

ACTOR 1. Was I doing you okay?

(Even though **LARRY** *has not clocked* **ACTOR 1**'s *performance at all...)*

LARRY. Very okay, actor [first name of Actor 1]!

ACTOR 1. So you were born here?

LARRY. Oh yeah! San Francisco, Jerry Rice, all the way!

ACTOR 1. I had no idea! For some reason I had imagined you with a stronger, accent?

LARRY. A accent?

LAUREN. I don't know why you would think that.

ACTOR 1. Just because when we were rehearsing, you said –

LAUREN. I didn't say that.

ACTOR 2. You kind of did.

LAUREN. I said like a Chinatown accent.

LARRY. A Chinatown accent?

ACTOR 1. Was I not doing that?

LAUREN. No. A Chinatown accent's more like –

ACTOR 1. Like what?

LAUREN. Like –

LARRY. Like a what?

LAUREN. Like –

> (**LAUREN** *coughs.*)

LARRY. You okay? You need some water?

LAUREN. I have water.

LARRY. *(Re: box.)* I got water in here.
  (To audience.) You want water?

LAUREN. They have water!

> *(They actually don't have water.)*

ACTOR 1. I would love some water.

ACTOR 2. Yeah, that'd be great.
  (To **LAUREN.***)* If that's okay.

LARRY. Yeah! Have some water!

> (**LARRY** *takes bottled water out of his cardboard
> box, hands it out to the* **ACTORS**, *maybe even
> the audience.*)

ACTOR 1. Thank you.

ACTOR 2. Thank you so much.

LAUREN. Yes. Great. Thank you, Daddy. So you good?

LARRY. I'm good, boss!

LAUREN. Maybe you should get back to your fundraiser.

LARRY. Oh, it ended early.

LAUREN. Then maybe you can wait downstairs while we continue –

ACTOR 2. You're making him leave?!

LARRY. That's okay, I'll just –

> (**LARRY** *gets up, takes a step. His ankle goes again.*)

Ohp, ohp! Hold on, hold on.

ACTOR 2. You should sit.

ACTOR 1. I mean, this is your club.

LAUREN. (*Re:* **LARRY** *in the middle of the stage.*) You don't really want him here, right?

ACTOR 1. We just act around him.

LARRY. Nooo, I gotta go soon. Joe Yu's coming by, in two minutes. Take me to the chiropractor. Gonna give me some herbs for my ankle.

LAUREN. Wouldn't that make him an herbalist?

LARRY. My chiropractor does everything! Got the weird beard.

LAUREN. What?

ACTOR 1. You're not gonna let him sit for two minutes?

LAUREN. Fine. Two minutes. Just until Joe Yu comes.

LARRY. Don't worry, boss. You won't even see me! It'll be like I'm not even here.

> (**LARRY** *grabs one of the signs from his box, holds it up, covers himself.*)

(*As if invisible/not here.*) What? What'd you say? I can't hear you 'cause I'm not here. "Who is it?" "Larry Yee, FBI!"

ACTOR 2. You work for the FBI?

LAUREN. He's a telephone man.

LARRY. But I could've!

"SECRET ASIAN MAN! SECRET ASIAN MAN!"

> (*As* **LARRY** *hums, he realizes he's holding up a Leland Yee campaign sign.*)

Hey. Yee!

(Re: sign.) You need a set? Here's a set.

LAUREN. That says "Leland" on it.

LARRY. "Leland Yee," "Lauren Yee." Pretty close.

ACTOR 2. Oh hey, "Leland Yee"!

LARRY. You know the senator?

ACTOR 2. No, but I've seen those signs everywhere on Nineteenth Avenue.

ACTOR 1. Oh yeah!

LARRY. I put those up yesterday, all over the Sunset District. *(To audience.)* California State Senator Dr. Leland Yee!

LAUREN. No relation.

LARRY. He's running for secretary of state! I've been working on his campaigns for almost twenty years!

ACTOR 2. Are you his campaign manager?

LAUREN. He's a volunteer.

LARRY. I am the volunteer.

LAUREN. It means he doesn't get paid.

LARRY. That's okay. Serve the community!

ACTOR 2. We don't get paid either!

ACTOR 1. And I'm Equity!

LARRY. Well, you ever need anything, just give us a call.

LAUREN. Welllllll –

LARRY. You watch our back, we'll scratch yours!

ACTOR 2. Oh, that's so nice.

LARRY. Chinese gotta stick together. Me and Leland's the same way. When Leland needs something done, I get it done! Everyone in Chinatown knows I'm Leland's sign guy. His hatchet man! *(Realizes.)* Ohp! Don't say that. Cut that. Off the record!

> *(Beat.)*

But he tells me everything! I'm a big supporter.

LAUREN. Just because he's a Yee.

LARRY. No.

(Beat.)

LARRY. Though also yes. Because I'm a Yee. And the senator's a Yee. Also because he's our cousin.

LAUREN. He's not our cousin.

LARRY. Sure he is. We all go back to the same Model Ancestor.

> *(Maybe there is a projector in the association. If so,* **LARRY** *takes out his slide clicker and we see a projection of the Model Ancestor portrait.)*

"Yee Fung Toy."

ACTOR 2. Oh, like the "Yee Fung Toy Family Association"!

LARRY. Yeah! He's the Yee who saved us when hundreds of years ago, we were being slaughtered.

ACTOR 1. Slaughtered?

LARRY. Well, back in the old days, if your clan fought and lost, the other side would slaughter you. There weren't too many Yees back then. We're not like the Wongs, we don't just grow on trees, you know. So when we were being slaughtered, the Model Ancestor knew he had to do something. So he brought us down to Southern China, so that nearly a thousand years later, we still exist.

ACTOR 1. Wow.

ACTOR 2. That's an amazing story!

LAUREN. Exactly: it's just a story.

LARRY. "Just a story"?!

LAUREN. It's not actually true. The Model Ancestor didn't actually exist.

LARRY. Oh yes, he did! I know it for a fact.

LAUREN. How?

LARRY. I remember!

LAUREN. 'Cause you were there?

LARRY. 'Cause my dad told me and his dad told him. And as long as someone remembers, it always remains true.

(Beat.)

Like how I am always on time.

LAUREN. You are never on time.

LARRY. But the more you say it, the more it comes true! "Where were you?" "Me? I was on time."

LAUREN. You were late to this. And you weren't even invited!

LARRY. *(To audience.)* The Model Ancestor is the first most famous Yee! There are three famous Yees you need to know!

LAUREN. You actually don't need to know this.

LARRY. *(Clicks through slides.)* You got the Model Ancestor, you got Leland –

(Slide of Lauren.)

And my daughter! Lauren Yee. *Ho leng ah!** Three! Three famous Yees.

(Like the Count in Sesame Street.*)* Ah ah ah.

LAUREN. Zwillinger.

LARRY. What?

LAUREN. Lauren Zwillinger.

LARRY. You changed it?

LAUREN. I finally got around to it.

LARRY. *(Can't pronounce.)* "Zerwillagur."

LAUREN. "Zwillinger."

LARRY. That's a lot of letters.

LAUREN. Well, that's my name now! Lauren Zwillinger.

LARRY. So two. Two famous Yees. Ah ah ah.

LAUREN. I thought Joe Yu was coming up. Two minutes ago.

LARRY. *(Checks phone.)* He's still looking for parking. Ohp! He found a space.

LAUREN. Great!

LARRY. Ohp! Now he needs to go look for change.

---

*So pretty!

LAUREN. It's Sunday.

LARRY. Yeah, but now they're charging.

ACTOR 2. Really?!

LARRY. I campaigned against it. Attacking the small businesses!

ACTOR 2. I gotta feed my meter!

LAUREN. Now?

LARRY. *(Checks phone.)* Joe Yu says the meter maid's coming around.

ACTOR 2. I'll be right back.

LARRY. You need change?

ACTOR 2. Do they not take credit cards?

LARRY. Take some money.

LAUREN. She doesn't need your money.

> *(**ACTOR 2** takes the change **LARRY** offers.)*

ACTOR 2. Thanks, Mr. Yee!

LAUREN. "Mr. Yee"?

ACTOR 2. That's his name, right?

LARRY. You can call me Larry.

ACTOR 2. Okay, Mr. Yee.

> *(**ACTOR 2** scurries off.)*

ACTOR 1. So what do you want to do now?

LARRY. Oooh, yeah, what's next?

ACTOR 1. 'Cause maybe I could show him the part where I –

LAUREN. Let's just wait.

ACTOR 1. Really?

LAUREN. Let's just wait till Joe Yu gets here and – *(Gestures to **LARRY**.)*

ACTOR 1. *(Slow on the uptake.)* Okay. Oh. Oh! 'Cause he's – *(To **LARRY**.)* She hasn't shown you the script yet?

LAUREN. No.

ACTOR 1. Ohhh.

> *(An awkward silence descends on them.)*

LARRY. *(To audience.)* Sooo any of you Yees out there?

LAUREN. They're not Yees.

LARRY. They look like Yees.

LAUREN. They're not Yees.

LARRY. Honorary Yees!

LAUREN. How can they be Yees? They're white. They're all white.

> (**LARRY** *finds the one Asian guy in the audience [***DANNY MA***].)*

LARRY. No, they are not. And him! He's a Yee!

LAUREN. Don't assume he's a Yee.

LARRY. Looks like a Yee! You a Yee?

DANNY MA. No?

LARRY. You sure?

LAUREN. *(To* **DANNY MA**.*)* I am so sorry, you do not have to answer that.

LARRY. What's your last name?

DANNY MA. Ma? Danny Ma?

LARRY. Ma. See? You're our cousin.

DANNY MA. Really?

LARRY. Oh yeah: the Mas, they're our cousins.

LAUREN. You're not our cousin.

LARRY. A long time ago, we had a Yee whose father died. His mother was a Ma, so the Mas took him in, and since then, we always acknowledge the Mas as our cousins.

DANNY MA. Yeah, but that may not even be my real last name.

LARRY. Ohhh, so "Ma" might be your paper name.

DANNY MA. Yeah.

LAUREN. What's a paper name?

LARRY. *(To audience.)* Well, "a paper name" is when you're Chinese and you come to America and you gotta get yourself some papers that say, "Oh yeah sure, I'm supposed to be here, yeah –"

DANNY MA. – When you're actually not!

LARRY. "Wink wink." And sometimes the fake papers got a different last name than your actual name. And the fake name is known as your "paper name." Most people keep the fake name, even though everyone else in Chinatown knows your real name. And that's basically the Chinese Excusion – Excludon? Clusion. *(Starts again.)* The Chinese "Don't Let Them In" Act of 1882!

DANNY MA. Exactly!

LAUREN. Daddy, we have no idea what you're talking about.

ACTOR 1. I got it.

LARRY. So you ask your dad about it?

DANNY MA. I never really knew my dad. We just have his last name.

LARRY. Either way, we can look it up.

DANNY MA. How?

LARRY. Just go over to the Ma Association, look it up.

LAUREN. Great, look it up. Look it up later.

DANNY MA. But I already went to the Mas. Nobody was there.

LARRY. Nobody was there? Or nobody answered the door?

DANNY MA. Nobody came when I knocked?

LARRY. You gotta know which door to knock on, which name to say.

DANNY MA. Really?!

LARRY. In Chinatown, you just need to know the magic words. We get one of the Mas to bring you in.

DANNY MA. Who?

LARRY. I introduce you to Frank Ma.

DANNY MA. That'd be great.

LARRY. You'll meet him at the dinner tonight.

DANNY MA. What dinner?

LARRY. She didn't tell you about the dinner?

DANNY MA. No.

LARRY. We're having a dinner tonight for my birthday. I'm turning sixty.

DANNY MA. Wow.

ACTOR 1. Congratulations, Mr. Yee! Big birthday!

LARRY. The biggest! You Chinese: sixty, it's the most important one!

LAUREN. They know what it means to turn sixty.

LARRY. Meant you lived through the whole zodiac!
The big caboodle!
Used to be you still alive at sixty, that was big stuff!
Any of your friends want to come to the dinner?

LAUREN. No.

DANNY MA. Sure!

LARRY. Call your parents! We bought out the whole restaurant for tonight!

ACTOR 1. Oh maybe.

LARRY. It's at New Asia. Everyone'll be there. You'll get to meet the senator.

ACTOR 1. My mom would love that. She always votes for Leland Yee.

LARRY. Because she's Chinese! And Chinatown votes together! It's our political machine! *(Stops.)* I mean, community machine! So what about you? You vote?

ACTOR 1. Nah.

LARRY. Why not?

ACTOR 1. I don't like jury duty.

LARRY. You gotta vote. Civic duty. You don't vote, who knows what could happen! Here, I'm registering voters for Leland.

LAUREN. Daddy, don't make him vote.

LARRY. You gotta vote. For the Chinese community.

> *(**LARRY** hands **ACTOR 1** a voter registration form.)*

ACTOR 1. Aaah, sure! Why not!

LAUREN. I thought you didn't want jury duty.

ACTOR 1. I guess I don't mind. *(Re: backstage.)* I'll fill it out back there.

LARRY. The senator appreciates your support.

ACTOR 1. Come get me when you're ready.

(**ACTOR 1** *exits to a backstage area.*)

LARRY. *(To audience.)* You a registered voter?

LAUREN. They're not here to become registered voters. Don't make them become registered voters.

(*But* **LARRY** *is already sending clipboards into the audience with* **DANNY MA.**)

LARRY. If it asks for the address, just put in uh, put in some address.

LAUREN. You can't do that.
(To audience.) Don't do that.

LARRY. Nobody'll check. Nobody ever checks! And when you're done with those, just give 'em to my assistant intern here.

DANNY MA. Aww.

LARRY. *(Gets a text.)* Oh, Joe Yu's downstairs! I better go grab him.

LAUREN. Great!

(**LARRY** *gets up, starts toward the door.*)

(To audience.) I'll just get the actors –

DANNY MA. Wait, Mr. Yee, before you go?

LARRY. Yeah?

DANNY MA. What do you think of your daughter's play?

LARRY. Aah, you don't want to ask me.

DANNY MA. But you're the president! This is your play.

LARRY. Me? No! It's my daughter's play.

DANNY MA. *(Re: program.)* "King of the Yees"?

LARRY. That's the title?

LAUREN. Working title.

DANNY MA. About you! *(Reads program.)* "Set in an obsolescent family association."

LARRY. Obso-what-scent?

DANNY MA. Obsolescent. In the process of becoming useless. Like the theater.

LAUREN. No, not like the theater.

LARRY. Hey, we're obsolescent, you're obsolescent, so what?

LAUREN. Maybe we should talk about something else.

> *(**LARRY** somehow now has a mic.)*

LARRY. Great! Who's next?

LAUREN. "Next"?

LARRY. We got a hand over there!

> *(**DANNY MA** runs the mic over to **JENNY PANG**.)*

What's your name and why're you calling?

JENNY PANG. Jenny Pang.

LARRY. *(Pretends not to hear.)* Who?

JENNY PANG. Jenny Pang!

> *(**LARRY** magically now has another mic. Where did that come from?)*

LARRY. Okay! Yeah! Jenny Pang, come on down!

> *(**JENNY PANG** doesn't know whether this means she should actually come on down, does something in between.)*

But first let me ask you one question, Jenny Pang: is your father Wilson Pang, one of my old co-workers?

JENNY PANG. He is!

LAUREN. How do you know that?

LARRY. She looks just like him!

*(To **JENNY PANG**.)* So how's your dad doing? How's his back?

JENNY PANG. Good! He told me to tell you – *"tong naw man hau ji ju."**

---

*Say hi to Spider for me.

LARRY. *Wilson nay ho.**

JENNY PANG. And also – *"gung hay coy toy yao."***

LAUREN. What?

JENNY PANG. *Tong naw man hau ji ju, gung hay coy toy yao.****

LARRY. Oh, you gotta say it in English. She doesn't understand.

LAUREN. It's not just that I don't understand –

JENNY PANG. *Nay goy noy hai jook sing?*****

LARRY. *Hai ah. Dan hai naw do hai.******

LAUREN. *(To audience.)* I don't know why they're speaking Chinese. This is not part of it.

JENNY PANG. *Mut nei ge joong mun gum ho gei? Yu sin sang!*******

LARRY. Wellll, I don't know about that.

LAUREN. What'd you say?

LARRY. Oh, she just said, "Hello."

JENNY PANG. And, "Happy retirement!"

LAUREN. Retirement?

LARRY. AT&T finally bought me out.

LAUREN. You didn't tell me that.

LARRY. So Jenny Pang, what's your problem?

JENNY PANG. I guess this is more of an opinion, and no offense, Mr. Yee –

LARRY. None taken, Jenny Pang!

JENNY PANG. But I'm still waiting for your daughter to tackle the bigger questions facing Chinatown.

LAUREN. Like what?

---

*Hi, Wilson.
**And wish him a happy retirement.
***Say hi to Spider for me, and wish him a happy retirement.
****Your daughter is an ABC?
*****Yeah, but so am I.
******But your Chinese is great, Mr. Yee!

JENNY PANG. The undocumented restaurant workers, the elder abuse, the SROs. None of her fliers were translated into Chinese.

LAUREN. So?

JENNY PANG. If she's not reaching out to the Chinese community, then who is she making this play for?

LARRY. *(Re: audience.)* Them! The Jews.

LAUREN. Daddy!

JENNY PANG. – But why isn't she confronting San Francisco's gentrification problems head-on? I mean, every day I'm seeing luxury high-rises being built right at the borders of Chinatown. I'm seeing us lose our cultural institutions: the Great Star, Empress of China –

LARRY. The food was never that good.

JENNY PANG. How can we stop what's happening in the Mission from happening in Chinatown? And how can we make sure we're taking care of *(Re: **LARRY**.)* our seniors!

LARRY. Not that much of a senior.

JENNY PANG. So Chinatown doesn't just became a playland for tourists and gangsters like *Ha Jai* –

LARRY. Shhh!

LAUREN. Who?

JENNY PANG. Shrimp Boy.

> *(Maybe there is thunder every time Shrimp Boy's name is said?)*

LARRY. Shhh!

LAUREN. What's a "Shrimp Boy"?

LARRY. Not so loud!

JENNY PANG. He runs the Ghee Kung Tong and everybody knows what that is.

LAUREN. I don't know what that is.

LARRY. You don't need to know what that is.

DANNY MA. I'd like to know what that is.

JENNY PANG. The Ghee Kung Tong. The gang.

LARRY. Or business "tong."

JENNY PANG. Right. "Tong." The Chinese word for "gang."

LARRY. Or just the Chinese word for "tong"!

JENNY PANG. He and his boys control Chinatown.

DANNY MA. So can we bring in this Shrimp Boy?

LARRY. You don't want to do that.

LAUREN. Why not?

> (**LARRY** *gestures to provide an example of why not.*)

JENNY PANG. These are exactly the kind of issues we haven't heard anything about so far.

DANNY MA. Well, maybe if you let Mr. Yee finish his presentation, he'd get to it.

JENNY PANG. His presentation.

DANNY MA. Yes, his.

JENNY PANG. Fine then, so will you? What do you think about all this?

LARRY. I think we got too much information here that nobody's gonna understand. Maybe we should move on –

LAUREN. Great! Let's move on.

JENNY PANG. And I'm also questioning the purpose of these associations. What are they doing for the community, except sitting on millions / of dollars –

LARRY. Shh sh sh sh!

JENNY PANG. Maybe even tens of millions of dollars!

LARRY. Or maybe just *(Small.)* "tens of millions of dollars."

JENNY PANG. What exactly does the Yee Fung Toy even do nowadays?

DANNY MA. Serve the Yee community!

LARRY. That's right, our cousin Danny Ma!

JENNY PANG. You mean the old, Chinese-speaking, male side of it.

DANNY MA. That's just who runs it, who's on the board.

JENNY PANG. But if women aren't even being elected to the board, how can they be fairly represented?

DANNY MA. Who says they can't be elected? Have these women even tried?

JENNY PANG. You have, right?

LAUREN. No?

DANNY MA. See? It doesn't even sound like she wants to join in the first place.

LARRY. *(Aside.)* Is this part of your play?

LAUREN. *(Aside.)* No.

JENNY PANG. But what about her kids? They can't join.

LAUREN. – I don't have any kids!

LARRY. Yet.

JENNY PANG. To me, this is the saddest part. She's standing right here in this association, talking about an organization that's never going to be talking to her or about her. And her poor kids –

DANNY MA. Well, excuse me, but I don't see any kids.

JENNY PANG. Yet.

    (To **LAUREN**.*)* Right?

LAUREN. Any other questions? Oh! I see a hand.

JENNY PANG. Where?

LAUREN. Back there.

> *(**JENNY PANG** grudgingly runs the mic into the back of the theater.)*

JENNY PANG. But I'm on your side –

LAUREN. Yep, keep keep, yep.

JENNY PANG. But what about Chinatown...?

> *(**SOMEONE** speaks. We don't see him. He has a slight Chinese accent.)*

SOMEONE. First-time guest: can you tell us about the doors?

LAUREN. That's actually a great question, uh –

SOMEONE. Raymond.

LAUREN. Raymond...last name?

SOMEONE. Just a Raymond.

LAUREN. Okay, "Just a Raymond"! Daddy?

LARRY. The doors are very important to us! They're almost a hundred fifty years old.

Some say they might be to keep the ghosts out.

Some say they might be to keep the ghosts in.

But what my dad told me – and what I believe – is that these doors link us to our ancestors: our father's father's father and our father's father and maybe even our dad.

DANNY MA. Do they ever open?

LARRY. Well, they're Yee doors, so they only open for Yees.

DANNY MA. *(Sad.)* Oh.

LARRY. And whenever you a Yee in need, all you gotta do is call on the ancestors to help these doors open up.

> *(Dramatic pause.)*

> *(To **LAUREN**.)* Open up –

LAUREN. What?

DANNY MA. "Open up."

> *(**LAUREN** tries to open the red double doors; they don't budge.)*

LAUREN. It's stuck.

LARRY. Just put some muscle into it, command 'em!

DANNY MA. Yeah, command 'em!

LAUREN. Daddy, they don't open.

LARRY. You a Yee, you can open it. The big caboodle. One more time, let's go!

> *(**LAUREN** tries again. Hard. It doesn't work.)*

LAUREN. I can't.

> *(**LAUREN** gives up.)*

LARRY. You haven't even tried! You just not doing it right.

LAUREN. Well, maybe I don't want to try if I'm already "not doing it right."

LARRY. 'Cause you would rather not do something than to do it incorrect?

LAUREN. Incorrectly, yes.

(To **SOMEONE**.*)* So does that answer your question, "Just a Raymond"?

(The **SOMEONE** *seems to have disappeared.)*

"Just a Raymond"? Where did he go?

LARRY. I see one more hand over there.

LAUREN. Where?

LARRY. Or maybe more like a paw –

LAUREN. A paw...?

(A paw pops out from behind the doors. A **LION DANCE** *bursts onstage. Clanging cymbals, giant drums. The* **LION DANCE** *wiggles around the room.)*

What is this?

LARRY. Looks like a lion dance.

LAUREN. But what is a lion dance doing here?

LARRY. Who knows! Maybe someone called a lion dance from the –

(To audience, an ad.) Foshan Mixed Martial Arts Studio on Jackson and Kearny! Good prices, youth classes, lots of fun.

LAUREN. Daddy?

LARRY. Yes?

LAUREN. There is no lion dance in this play!

LARRY. But then what do you want to do with the erhu player?

LAUREN. What erhu player?

*(***LAUREN** *hears/sees an* **ERHU PLAYER**.*)*

You've got to be kidding me!

LARRY. No, it really is the world-famous Dr. Zhao, erhu player!

ERHU PLAYER. *(To audience.) Lo fan nay ho.**

LARRY. *(To audience.)* What do we want?

ALL. *(But mostly* **DANNY MA** *and* **LARRY***.)* Yee!

LARRY. When do we want it?

ALL. *(But mostly* **DANNY MA** *and* **LARRY***.)* Yee!
   Yee Yee Yee Yee! /
   Yee Yee Yee Yee!

LAUREN. Okay, hi. Hi. Hi. Hi. Hi there, hi.

> (**ERHU PLAYER** *stops playing.* **LION DANCE** *also stops.)*

I'm sorry –

LARRY. Dr. Zhao and the world-famous Foshan Lion Dance!

> *(Claps.)*

LAUREN. Yes, thank you for coming –

LARRY. Thanks, Joe.

LAUREN. But we can't afford this.

LARRY. Don't worry. We already rented them for the dinner tonight. Imma give your supporters a sneak peek! Let 'em see the lion do the cabbage.

DANNY MA. Oooh.

LAUREN. The what?

LARRY. He pretends to eat the cabbage and then he spits it back out at the people.

DANNY MA. It's great.

> *(The* **LION DANCE** *nods: "Yeah! I got a cabbage!")*

LAUREN. Sure, but I don't think they *(Re: audience.)* want this right now.

LARRY. *(To audience.)* You sure? You want this?

> (**LARRY***, the* **LION DANCE***, and the* **ERHU PLAYER** *look toward the audience appealingly.*

---

*Hello, white people.

> *Actually, they kind of would not mind seeing more of this.)*

They want this! All in favor? Aye!

DANNY MA. Aye!

ERHU PLAYER. *Ho!**

> (**LARRY**, **DANNY MA**, *the* **LION DANCE**, *the* **ERHU PLAYER**, *and maybe even some of the audience raise their hands.)*

LARRY. We let 'em hang around till the face changer gets here.

LAUREN. The what?!

LARRY. We got a Sichuan face changer coming.

DANNY MA. Oooh!

LAUREN. What is that?

LARRY. The guy with the face.

> (**LARRY** *makes a hand/face gesture that provides us with no information.)*

He does it real fast.

LAUREN. Daddy, come here.

LARRY. You need something?

LAUREN. Yes.

> *(To* **DANNY MA**.*)* Go get the actors.

DANNY MA. I don't know where they are.

LAUREN. I'm sure they're right back there.

DANNY MA. Okay, but I don't actually work here.

> (**LAUREN** *tries to get* **LARRY** *offstage.)*

LAUREN. Daddy, let's go.

LARRY. Where?

LAUREN. Over here.

LARRY. Okay, boss!

> *(To audience.)* Welcome to "King of the Yees"!

---

*Aye!

LAUREN. They're already here. You don't need to say welcome if they're already here.

LARRY. You already say welcome?

LAUREN. Um –

DANNY MA. No.

LARRY. You gotta welcome them. They're here to support you.

LAUREN. I'll be right back, but in the meantime "welcome to King of the / Yees."

LARRY. What?

LAUREN. King of the –

LARRY. Can't hear you!

LAUREN. King of the Yees!

LARRY. And on with the show!

> (**LARRY** *gestures. In response, a gong sounds.* **LAUREN** *looks around. Where is that gong coming from?! Might be* **DANNY MA** *with the gong. The* **LION DANCE** *and* **ERHU PLAYER** *continue.* **LAUREN** *pushes* **LARRY** *offstage.*)

Hallway

*(**ACTOR 2** is listening against the door. **ACTOR 1** fills out a voter registration form.)*

ACTOR 2. You sure they're not waiting for us?

ACTOR 1. She said she'll come get us.

ACTOR 2. I want to give Mr. Yee back his change.

ACTOR 1. Then you go out and check.

ACTOR 2. You want to run lines at least?

ACTOR 1. Relax, we're on break.

ACTOR 2. *(Sighs, then.)* So while we're out here, can I ask –

ACTOR 1. Ask!

ACTOR 2. What I don't get –

ACTOR 1. What don't you get?

ACTOR 2. It's a men's club?

ACTOR 1. It's a men's club.

ACTOR 2. For Chinese people. Named Yee.

ACTOR 1. Right.

> *(Beat.)*

Sorry, what don't you get?

ACTOR 2. I guess my question is why.

ACTOR 1. Why you'd want a men's club?

ACTOR 2. Why you'd want to save it.

ACTOR 1. So in the future you can have an association of Yee men...for some reason.

ACTOR 2. I should've asked when we were rehearsing.

ACTOR 1. Why didn't you?

ACTOR 2. If I ask, then I'm the one asking and I feel like she came in expecting us to know.

ACTOR 1. Just because we're Chinese.

ACTOR 2. *(Sly.)* Actually, I'm Korean.

ACTOR 1. Waaaah?

ACTOR 2. Don't don't – now you're going to get me in trouble!

ACTOR 1. For being Korean?

ACTOR 2. "King of the Yees."

ACTOR 1. So?

ACTOR 2. I had no idea the whole thing was going to be so Chinese-centric. I figured they were just looking for general Asians.

ACTOR 1. Well, fuck that. Fuck her.

ACTOR 2. Thank you.

ACTOR 1. Hey, I'm only three-quarters Chinese.

ACTOR 2. Really?!

ACTOR 1. My mother's mother was Irish.

ACTOR 2. Ohhhh, now I can see it.

ACTOR 1. It's like part of me is oppressing the rest of myself!

ACTOR 2. Could she tell you're not full Asian?

ACTOR 1. No! She can't tell. Even Asian people can't tell.

ACTOR 2. I'm so relieved, though, I didn't have to do my Chinese accent.

ACTOR 1. Why?

ACTOR 2. Mine is so bad.

ACTOR 1. Most Asians have awful Asian accents.

ACTOR 2. My Chinese is particularly bad.

ACTOR 1. Well, if you're Korean…

ACTOR 2. I had to do it one time for an audition.

ACTOR 1. And?

ACTOR 2. And they were just like, "Thank you! So great."

ACTOR 1. And you booked it?

ACTOR 2. And I booked it.

(They high five.)

ACTOR 1. So it couldn't have been that bad.

ACTOR 2. No, but mine was like – *(Accent.)* We are Chinese! We are Chinese!

ACTOR 1. *(Tries to help show example.)* We are Chinese!

ACTOR 2. Chinese!

ACTOR 1. *(Tries to help.)* Chiiiii chiiii –

ACTOR 2. Chiiii –

ACTOR 1. Chiiiiiinese!

ACTOR 2. Chiiiiiinese!

> *(Beat.)*

How was that? Was that Chinese?

ACTOR 1. ("That wasn't very good.") Mmm...

ACTOR 2. Somebody told me what you need to do is keep your mouth slack – *(Demonstrates.)* So that when you talk –

ACTOR 1. No.

ACTOR 2. No?

ACTOR 1. What my voice teacher said is that you do want to slack your jaw but you also want to keep the pressure on your diaphragm.

> *(**ACTOR 1** maybe helps with some physical adjustments.)*

Down here.

ACTOR 2. *(Tries this.)* Chinese.

ACTOR 1. You're hitting more of the "–nese" instead of the "Chi–."

ACTOR 2. Chinese.

ACTOR 1. Like you've been punched in the gut. Chinese.

ACTOR 2. Chinese.

ACTOR 1. Working in a rice paddy.

ACTOR 2. Chinese.

ACTOR 1. And there're bombs and Agent Orange raining down on you –

ACTOR 2. Then you're just doing Vietnamese.

ACTOR 1. No, wait. *(Corrects.)* There're Japanese bombs raining down on you –

ACTOR 2. *(Various, increasingly intense takes.)* Chinese!

ACTOR 1. And you can't see over your conical hat and your eyes are really small.

ACTOR 2. Chinese!

ACTOR 1. So you have to lean forward to see but you're still running from the Japanese bombs.

ACTOR 2. Chinese!

ACTOR 1. As the weight of all your ancestors is on the lower part of your diaphragm –

ACTOR 2. Chinese!

ACTOR 1. And the expectations of your unborn ABC children are pressing down on the back of your throat –

ACTOR 2. Chinese!

ACTOR 1. But from the inside, and you speak like there is a sorrow –

ACTOR 2. Chinese!

ACTOR 1. Buried so deeply inside of you *(Diaphragm.)* here and *(Throat.)* here –

ACTOR 2. Chinese!

ACTOR 1. Flatten the r's!

ACTOR 2. Chinese!

ACTOR 1. Watch your tones!

ACTOR 2. Chinese!

ACTOR 1. Dim sum carts!

ACTOR 2. Chinese!

ACTOR 1. Lactose intolerance!

ACTOR 2. Chinese!

ACTOR 1. Chinese!

ACTOR 2. Chinese!

ACTOR 1. Chinese!

ACTOR 2. Chinese!

ACTOR 1. Chinese!

ACTOR 2. Chinese!

      (Beat. They reflect on this.)

ACTOR 1. That's basically what Chinese people sound like. And my voice teacher spent two years living in Shanghai, so she knows.

ACTOR 2. That's really helpful. Thank you.

ACTOR 1. It takes work. Especially if you're Korean.

ACTOR 2. And adopted.

ACTOR 1. And adopted!

ACTOR 2. For Korean, what you have to do is just imagine that you're a woman – which for me is easy – and that Japanese oppressors are pillaging everything in sight, and you want to scream, but you've just had plastic surgery, so you can't move your face.

ACTOR 1. Korean!

ACTOR 2. Korean!

ACTOR 1. Korean!

(**ACTOR 1***'s Korean accent is not that good.*)

ACTOR 2. You'll probably never need it anyway.

Yee Fung Toy

(**LAUREN** *and* **LARRY** *in the stairway. The distant sound of lion dance.*)

LAUREN. Daddy –

LARRY. *(Checks phone.)* The face changer's on his way. He had to park all the way up on Mason. You want him to bring his magic, too?

LAUREN. Daddy, this is it, okay?

LARRY. What?

LAUREN. There are no lion dances, there are no erhu players.

LARRY. Not even a face changer?

LAUREN. Definitely not a face changer.

LARRY. You get a face changer, he can play all the parts. He already comes with all the faces.

LAUREN. No. And as soon as that lion dance is over, that's it, okay?

LARRY. But you love lion dance! You used to take lessons.

LAUREN. You signed me up so you could go off and hang up more signs for Leland.

LARRY. So you could learn something!

LAUREN. I couldn't understand anything. All the lessons were in Chinese!

LARRY. That is what we call a win-win. And your audience, they loved it!

LAUREN. But did you also have to mention the Model Ancestor, your chiropractor –?

LARRY. He's real good. Got the weird beard.

LAUREN. What does that even mean?

LARRY. And the Lum Elders! I forgot to mention the Lum Elders. They run Chinatown, their grandkids go to Lowell. I told 'em you'd talk to 'em about college.

LAUREN. Why did you promise them that?

LARRY. Oh! And the liquor store! Gotta mention them, too.

LAUREN. Why?

LARRY. They sponsored the alcohol for the dinner tonight. For free!

LAUREN. No, they didn't.

LARRY. Oh yes they did!

It's the place left on Washington, right on Grant.

The store with the red awning.

You gotta ask 'em for the good cheap stuff.

(Recapping.) So we got my chiropractor with the weird beard, the Lum Elders, the liquor store, the lion dance, the face changer –

LAUREN. Is there anyone else you need to thank?

LARRY. I'll write you down a list.

LAUREN. Daddy, I wrote this as a two-hander. Do you know what that means?

LARRY. Yeah. *(Re: two hands.)* You got the left and you got the right.

LAUREN. It means there are two actors in this play.

Because I am trying to tell the story of two people.

And you're trying to make it about everyone else.

LARRY. Hey, you doing a play about Chinatown?

LAUREN. Yes?

LARRY. And you gonna do it with two characters?

LAUREN. Uh-huh.

LARRY. That is a tall order, boss.

LAUREN. It's a play. Plays have two actors.

LARRY. But you talking about Chinatown, you gotta mention the whole community, make sure you telling the story for them instead of telling the story for them.

LAUREN. That is the exact same thing.

LARRY. No, there is telling the story for them and then there is telling the story for them.

LAUREN. What about the story am I not getting right?

LARRY. Chinatown is obso-what-scent?

LAUREN. "Obsolescent."

LARRY. Dead.

LAUREN. Dying.

LARRY. We got all those people to thank and Chinatown is dying?

LAUREN. Chinatown exists because a hundred fifty years ago, Chinese people couldn't live anywhere else. You grew up in Chinatown because you had to. I didn't. And isn't that what we call a win-win?

LARRY. Still your community, your people!

LAUREN. In twenty years of helping out Chinatown, all the time you spent here, with them, what has your community given you?

LARRY. Hey, when Leland makes secretary of state, he'll get me a position in the government, make me a big shot.

LAUREN. You said that when he made supervisor.

LARRY. Yeah?

LAUREN. When he made assembly, when he made state senate.

LARRY. If he'd just made mayor –

LAUREN. If he'd made mayor, he'd do the same thing he's done for twenty years, which is use you.

LARRY. Ah, I don't mind.

LAUREN. You should.

LARRY. I like being used. Makes me feel useful. I got use! I got power!

LAUREN. People taking advantage of you is not power.

LARRY. I'm the guy they call when they need something done.

LAUREN. When they need money. Whenever Leland needs to raise money, that's when he calls and he never thanks you.

LARRY. That's not true.

LAUREN. Today at the fundraiser: did he even thank you?

LARRY. Leland didn't come.

LAUREN. To his own fundraiser?

LARRY. But everyone else was there!

LAUREN. So you threw a fundraiser for a man who didn't even show up?

LARRY. Leland's been busy.

LAUREN. Or he doesn't respect you.

LARRY. The election's heating up. This Italian's come into the race. Big money.

LAUREN. Leland has money.

LARRY. But we gotta get more. Signs cost money. Commercials cost money. Making sure they remember your name: it all costs something.

LAUREN. So you let him take and take and take.

LARRY. Or I give and give and give.

LAUREN. That's the same thing.

LARRY. No, it is not!

> *(Beat.)*

I support Leland no matter what. He's my community. So if Imma hang up signs for Leland, I gotta retire.

LAUREN. You retired because of Leland?

LARRY. AT&T wouldn't let me take off work to hang up signs. They said, you want us to fire you? So I said, no, Imma retire. And now I go hang up all the signs I want!

LAUREN. For one election.

LARRY. This is a very important time. We need Leland, make sure we protect ourselves.

LAUREN. Against what?

LARRY. Whoever's gonna try to knock us off our branch!

LAUREN. Daddy, that's not going to happen.

LARRY. You don't have use, you don't have power? They will erase you from your own story.

LAUREN. Our family has been in America for how long? – A hundred, hundred fifty years?

LARRY. And now you're going to Germany. My daughter, so full of surprises!

LAUREN. I should've mentioned it to you and Mom, yes.

LARRY. How you gonna learn German when you don't even know Chinese?

LAUREN. Germans speak English. They make it a priority.

LARRY. And Zach's Jewish.

LAUREN. So?

LARRY. You go there, you are asking for trouble.

LAUREN. Daddy, you know nothing about Jews!

LARRY. I know enough.

LAUREN. What, what do you know?

LARRY. They got the hats. And the –

>   (**LARRY** *makes a cryptic, non-Jewish-specific gesture.*)

Do they even got a Chinatown there?

LAUREN. I don't need a Chinatown. Especially when Chinatown doesn't seem to want me.

LARRY. What makes you think that?

LAUREN. I don't know this place, I don't speak the language.

LARRY. Hey, when I was your age, neither did I! But I learned, for the association. And so can you!

LAUREN. No, I can't!

LARRY. Do it for your kids!

LAUREN. We don't have kids! And who knows if we ever will!

>   (*Beat.*)

You knew that, right?

LARRY. I, uh –

LAUREN. I mean, who says I have to have kids? Who says I have to continue something just because it's been going on for years and years?

LARRY. Thirty-six generations.

LAUREN. I don't have to decide now. I'm young.

LARRY. You're thirty.

LAUREN. Okay, I came all this way, I'm missing my reading in New York tomorrow so I could come and celebrate your birthday. Sixty! One whole life.

LARRY. One whole life.

LAUREN. So let's enjoy this.

LARRY. You should go back, go see it.

LAUREN. I already bought my flight.

LARRY. Change it, go home, forget about the dinner.

LAUREN. American Airlines isn't gonna let me just change my flight.

LARRY. Sure they will! My chiropractor: his daughter works for American. I got her brother a job at the fortune cookie factory. You need a change, she'll do it for free.

LAUREN. Is that what you want?

LARRY. Come, don't come. As long as we fill up the tables.

LAUREN. Of course I'm coming.

> (**LARRY** *takes out his phone.*)

LARRY. I gotta make a call.

LAUREN. See you at the dinner?

LARRY. *(On phone.)* Uh-huh.

> (**LAUREN** *exits.* **LARRY** *lowers the phone, just stands there.*)

Hallway

ACTOR 2. Do you want kids?

ACTOR 1. I have a kid.

ACTOR 2. What?!

ACTOR 1. My daughter. She's eight.

>   (**ACTOR 1** *shows her a picture of his daughter on his phone.*)

ACTOR 2. Awww. And you're an actor?

ACTOR 1. Her mom's a cardiologist.

ACTOR 2. Smart.

ACTOR 1. Thank you!

ACTOR 2. *(Re: photo.)* Is your daughter –?

ACTOR 1. Mixed. Obviously.

ACTOR 2. Mixed kids are the way of the future.

ACTOR 1. She's got a Chinese last name, so she can whip out Asian whenever she wants.

ACTOR 2. I feel like the ideal name is white first name, white last name, but Asian middle name so you can blend in when necessary, but you can also be like, "Ethnic minority, bitch!" That's what I would want, if I wanted kids.

ACTOR 1. You don't want kids?

ACTOR 2. I never want kids.

ACTOR 1. Do you not like kids?

ACTOR 2. I like kids. I like my brother's kid. And that's enough for me. Come in, cool aunt, birthdays, Halloween, that's all I need.

ACTOR 1. But what'll you do when you get old?

ACTOR 2. What do you mean?

ACTOR 1. Who's going to take care of you when you fall down and hurt yourself?

ACTOR 2. Shoot, I'm getting Life Alert. Imma be one of those grannies in the commercials. I'll be falling and then be like, "Boom, rescue me, bitch!"

ACTOR 1. Lot of bitches in your fantasies.

ACTOR 2. It's for impact. And effect.

ACTOR 1. But then who's going to be sad for you when you're gone?

ACTOR 2. Hey, who says if I have kids, they're going to be sad for me when I'm gone?

ACTOR 1. Ouch.

ACTOR 2. I could give up acting, have kids, and they could still hate me and move to – where is she moving to?

ACTOR 1. Berlin.

ACTOR 2. Berlin! And that'd be worse 'cause then I gave up acting and all my grandkids are German. *(Stops.)* Your daughter will be sad, though, after you're gone.

ACTOR 1. I hope so.

ACTOR 2. She will.

ACTOR 1. Not her whole life, not cripplingly so, but every so often. Like on my birthday. I'd like that.

ACTOR 2. Like, *(As sad daughter, German accent.)* "*Ja, mein Father*. How I miss him."

ACTOR 1. Exactly. That's exactly what I want.

Yee Fung Toy

(**LARRY** *back in the meeting room.*)

LARRY. *(To audience.)* My daughter told me to tell you she'll be right back.

She also told me I'm not supposed to tell you anything else, so – ("zip!")

I gotta go soon anyway, get ready for the dinner, find the Doc.

That's Leland.

He calls me Larry.

I call him the Doc.

We're pretty tight.

I remember the first election I did with Leland. Supervisor's race.

He called me up, night before the election, and he told me, "Larry, you gotta go down to the Sunset District, take down all those other guys' signs, and put up mine."

So I said, "Okay, Doc. Don't you worry.

(As Yogi Bear.) Larry Yee is on the case!"

And the next day,

All of Nineteenth Avenue, the whole Sunset District is just "Yee,"

One after the other.

"Yee,"

"Yee,"

"Yee."

I'm not saying I won it for him, but my dad always used to say, having your name up there, that's pretty important.

> *(Bang!)*
>
> *(Where is that coming from? The red double doors?)*

Lauren?

No?

Who is it?

"Larry Yee: FBI!"

> *(An unseen old TV mounted in the ceiling corner turns on.* **LARRY** *looks up.)*

Oh hey, Channel Four, they've got Leland. We made the afternoon news!

Hey, Doc!

Wonder where he is.

And look! The association! They got a picture of us! Wow.

> *(***LARRY*** *takes out a remote.)*

Lemme turn up the volume.

> *(***LARRY*** *turns up the volume. News footage…)*

CHORUS. *(***ACTORS 1, 2 & 3** *taking alternate lines/paragraphs.)*
Breaking news
Breaking news
Sudden, shocking allegations.

LARRY. Huh?

CHORUS. Leland Yee
The Chinese American state senator currently running for
Formerly running for
Arrested by the FBI
Indicted this afternoon
On charges of public corruption
Arms trafficking
And bribery.

LARRY. Bribery? No! The Doc doesn't need the money. He's too smart for that!

CHORUS. After a failed mayoral bid
His first political defeat in over twenty years
Senator Yee was caught on a wiretap
Telling undercover agents –

LELAND. "Do I think we can make some money? I think we can make some money. Do I think we can get the goods? I think we can get the goods."

CHORUS. Demanding "pay to play" money in order to raise funds for his upcoming secretary of state race.

LARRY. Oh wow.

CHORUS. Will Leland Yee's indictment negatively impact the good name of other Yees?

Betty Yee, currently running for California state comptroller, issued a statement:

BETTY YEE. "I am not and have never been a part of Leland Yee's circle. We are not related. It's just a name, guys."

CHORUS. Betty Yee's campaign manager Parke Skelton added this odd remark:

PARKE SKELTON. "If Betty was a senator named Larry Yee, I'd be more concerned."

CHORUS. Potentially referencing recently laid-off telephone worker

Former future grandfather

And local obsolescent organization president

(*All.*) Larry Yee.

> (**LARRY** *loses all color.*)

LARRY. I should, uh –

This is not –

I don't know what this is.

And I gotta get ready for the dinner.

We got fifty tables coming.

Everyone'll be there.

Everyone'll be there.

> (*Bang!*)
>
> (*Bang!*)
>
> (*Bang!*)
>
> (**LARRY** *turns and opens the red double doors.*)

CHORUS. When contacted for comment on the senator's arrest

Larry Yee...

> (**LARRY** *steps through the doors.*)

...Could not be found.

> (*The red double doors slam shut.* **LAUREN** *enters.*)

LAUREN. Daddy? Daddy?

End of Act One

ACT TWO

Hallway

(**ACTOR 1** *looks at his phone.*)

ACTOR 1. Whoa.

ACTOR 2. What?

ACTOR 1. Leland Yee's in jail.

ACTOR 2. Really?!

ACTOR 1. The FBI just took him in. Wow.

ACTOR 2. I hope she's okay.

ACTOR 1. Who?

ACTOR 2. Lauren.

ACTOR 1. Lauren?

ACTOR 2. Her dad just got arrested.

ACTOR 1. Her dad's Larry Yee. The senator is Leland Yee.

ACTOR 2. Okay, too many Yees.

ACTOR 1. We just saw Mr. Yee. How could he be in jail if we just saw him?

ACTOR 2. We saw him, what, five, ten, twenty minutes ago? For all we know, he could be in jail right now and we'd have no idea. Maybe that's why she hasn't come out for us yet.

ACTOR 1. Nah, they just went after Leland and Shrimp Boy.

ACTOR 2. Who?

ACTOR 1. Shrimp Boy.

ACTOR 2. Should I know who that is?

ACTOR 1. You live here. How do you not know this? He runs Chinatown.

ACTOR 2. I'm Korean. And adopted.

ACTOR 1. Oh, right.

ACTOR 2. So why is he called Shrimp Boy? Is he a midget?

ACTOR 1. That's just his name.

ACTOR 2. It doesn't exactly inspire fear.

ACTOR 1. Maybe it sounds scarier in Chinese. *"Ha Jai."* *(Scary.)* *"Ha Jai."*

ACTOR 2. He should change it.

ACTOR 1. He will kill you for saying that.

ACTOR 2. Isn't he being held by the FBI?

ACTOR 1. *(Checks phone.)* No. Leland's in jail, you-know-who's still on the loose.

ACTOR 2. Oh shoot.

ACTOR 1. How do you not know him? I don't even live here anymore and I know him.

ACTOR 2. You live in New York?

ACTOR 1. LA.

ACTOR 2. I love LA!

ACTOR 1. Good for you.

ACTOR 2. Sometimes I'm like, I should just move there, you know?

ACTOR 1. You should! – I mean, don't. It's awful, but – you should!

ACTOR 2. And Rodney Chen he was telling me – do you know Rodney Chen?

ACTOR 1. Just because he's Asian?

ACTOR 2. And an actor.

ACTOR 1. Oh, no, Rodney Chen. I do. I do know him.

ACTOR 2. See, all the Asians know each other.

ACTOR 1. So racist.

ACTOR 2. So true.

ACTOR 1. So how do you know Rodney Chen?

ACTOR 2. Around. We're still friends. Weirdly enough.

ACTOR 1. Oh, that's how you know Rodney Chen.

ACTOR 2. Never happened.

ACTOR 1. No?

ACTOR 2. "If I don't remember, then it never happened." Just like Mr. Yee said!

ACTOR 1. I don't think he meant it like that.

ACTOR 2. But anyway, Rodney was telling me you can go to LA and pick up work pretty quickly as an Asian.

ACTOR 1. Rodney Chen lies.

ACTOR 2. Really?

ACTOR 1. Asian actors go to LA and they just disappear.

ACTOR 2. What?!

ACTOR 1. You can audition and audition, years go by, and it's like you were never there at all.
(Chinese accent.) You try, you try, but no work come back to you!

ACTOR 2. *(Chinese accent.)* No work come back to you!

ACTOR 1. Chiiiinese.

ACTOR 2. Chiiiinese.

ACTOR 1. Better!

ACTOR 2. Really?

ACTOR 1. Totally getting better.

ACTOR 2. Thanks, teach!

Yee Fung Toy

*(**LAUREN** on the phone, pacing the room.)*

LAUREN. No, Zach, I searched the building, I searched the block, I searched all over Chinatown.

Nothing.

He's disappeared.

…

What do you mean, "Did I ask anyone in Chinatown"?

Of course not.

How would I possibly do that?

…

Or the FBI has him.

Or he's out destroying evidence for Leland.

(Something begins to happen with the red double doors.)

No, I came back and he was gone. The whole room was empty except for –

*(**LAUREN** sees the doors, the hint of magic.)*

– These red double doors.

*(**LAUREN** shakes off this vision.)*

No, I know: "If he's not on the news, then he's probably fine."

No, you're right.

Okay.

*(**LAUREN** hangs up. She faces the doors.)*

"Open sesame!"

"Alikazaam!"

"Open dóor."

(Nothing happens.)

Guess you do only open for Yees, huh?

CHORUS. – And yet, the whereabouts of one of Senator Yee's accomplices

(**LAUREN** *looks up at the TV.*)

Raymond

"Shrimp Boy"

Chow

"Dragonhead" of one of Chinatown's most notorious tongs

Still remain unknown.

> (*A figure emerges, the* **SOMEONE** *from earlier:* **SHRIMP BOY**. *Maybe he wears a white Armani suit, beret, and sunglasses. Or maybe a red silk outfit. He accidentally spooks* **LAUREN**.)

LAUREN. Aaaah!

SHRIMP BOY. Oh. Sorry.

LAUREN. That's okay, [first name of Actor 1].

> (**SHRIMP BOY**'s *English is a little choppy. He's got a Hong Kong accent.*)

SHRIMP BOY. [Actor 1]? No [Actor 1] here.

LAUREN. Haha, very funny, [Actor 1]. Great costume by the way.

SHRIMP BOY. Costume? No costume.

You're Larry's daughter. You write the play. The movie?

LAUREN. Sorry, I just need to call the police, long story.

> (*Before* **LAUREN** *can dial,* **SHRIMP BOY** *shoots the phone out of her hand. He has excellent aim.*)

Aaaah!

SHRIMP BOY. You a stool pigeon, you die a stool pigeon.

LAUREN. Who are you?

> (**DANNY MA** *enters with a tapioca drink.*)

DANNY MA. Oh hey, where's Mr. Yee?

> (**SHRIMP BOY** *points the gun at* **DANNY MA**.)

SHRIMP BOY. Sit down.

DANNY MA. I'm just here for my phone.

SHRIMP BOY. Sit down.

> (**SHRIMP BOY** *raises his gun at* **DANNY MA.**)

DANNY MA. I'm not a Yee.

LAUREN. Though he is a cousin!

DANNY MA. I'm a Ma.

SHRIMP BOY. See! You a cousin.

LAUREN. Take a seat...coz.

DANNY MA. Who are you?

SHRIMP BOY. You ever hear of the famous shrimp?

> (*Maybe some thunder?*)

Yee Fung Toy

(One hour later. **SHRIMP BOY** *has* **LAUREN** *and* **DANNY MA** *as his hostages.* **SHRIMP BOY** *has been talking for a while. He sips Danny Ma's tapioca drink.)*

SHRIMP BOY. Chinatown, San Francisco. Back then Chinatown is very different. When you pull out a machine gun, shit is kicking off, getting serious. Pretty much everyone packing in Chinatown.
(To **LAUREN.***)* We'd go to bed with seven girls.
(Realizes, turns to **DANNY MA** *instead.)* We'd go to bed with seven girls. Ain't that fun? I mean, can you handle seven girls?

DANNY MA. *(Cries.)* No!

SHRIMP BOY. No. But you try!

DANNY MA. Please don't kill us!

SHRIMP BOY. Kill you? No! Imma inspire you.

LAUREN. What?

DANNY MA. You are?

SHRIMP BOY. Yeah! *(Checks watch.)* I gotta finish my story, inspire you before the FBI come arrest me, try to paint me as the criminal. But they don't know: I got Larry's daughter, the great Chinese screen movie writer who's gonna help me tell my story!

LAUREN. I am?

SHRIMP BOY. Oh yeah. Is very important! First time I go to jail, I do time with Charles Manson, a good friend of mine. Kimball, a serial killer. They say, "Raymond, you gotta tell your story, is the most important thing." You don't tell your story, the *lo fan* –

DANNY MA. That means "white person."

SHRIMP BOY. – Gonna tell it for you. Make you disappear in your own story! They tell me, "Raymond, you gotta make like the Jew."

LAUREN. Excuse me?!

DANNY MA. The Jew.

LAUREN. What do you have against Jewish people?

SHRIMP BOY. Oh no! I love the Jew. Imma big fan of their work!

LAUREN. Huh?

SHRIMP BOY. They just like us!

    The hard work,

    The good food,

    The can't see,

    The cheap skate,

    The mom so loud, always control the son.

    The dad bad at sport, cannot throw the ball.

    And now: the story!

DANNY MA. Ohhhh.

SHRIMP BOY. The Jew know you gotta stick together, make sure they don't erase you from your own story. Which is why I got you!

DANNY MA. *(Question.)* But out of everyone out there, you chose her.

SHRIMP BOY. Hey, she's Chinese and the Chinese gotta stick together!

DANNY MA. But then what am I here for?

SHRIMP BOY. You the youth, you gonna be inspire by my story.

DANNY MA. Okay.

SHRIMP BOY. You the youth and you the story.

LAUREN. Yes, I would love to help, but first I gotta find my dad.

SHRIMP BOY. Oh yeah, your dad, you break his heart, you gotta find him.

DANNY MA. Whaaaat?

LAUREN. No, I did not / break his –

DANNY MA. What did you do to Mr. Yee?

SHRIMP BOY. She don't want the kids.

DANNY MA. Ever?

LAUREN. I didn't say "never." I mean, why do I need to decide now? I'm thirty.

SHRIMP BOY. Exactly! You thirty.

DANNY MA. Tick tick tick.

SHRIMP BOY. You don't have the kids, you move to Germany –

DANNY MA. Oy.

LAUREN. It's a good job for Zach.

SHRIMP BOY. – And what you gonna miss with your dad?

LAUREN. My dad is sixty. I have time.

SHRIMP BOY. You sure about that?

DANNY MA. *(Sad.)* Tick tick tick.

SHRIMP BOY. When I am in jail, my mom come visit, say, "Raymond, why you go to jail so much, why you don't come see me?" And I say, "Ma, you embarrass me in front of good friend Chuck Manson!" And she say, "Raymond, why you don't get out on parole, come see me?" "I can't do it, Ma! I try so hard to be the best and still not enough! You put the pressure on me, you make me want to kill the people, steal the money!" Next week, she pass away!

DANNY MA. Aw.

SHRIMP BOY. She get sick, she don't even tell me!

DANNY MA. *(Nods.)* Chinese.

SHRIMP BOY. How much time you think you got?

LAUREN. But I looked all over Chinatown, he's gone.

SHRIMP BOY. You ask the chiropractor?

LAUREN. Which chiropractor?

SHRIMP BOY. The one with the weird beard.

> *(Beat.)*

DANNY MA. Ohhhh, that guy.

SHRIMP BOY. He knows all!

LAUREN. Well, I have no idea how to find a weird beard.

SHRIMP BOY. Okay. I help.

LAUREN. Really?!

DANNY MA. Yay.

SHRIMP BOY. You help me tell my story, I get my boys to find you your dad back.

LAUREN. Thank you.

(**LAUREN** *and* **SHRIMP BOY** *shake hands.*)

SHRIMP BOY. So now we get caught, we all go down same.

LAUREN. Excuse me?

SHRIMP BOY. Now you part of my gang.

LAUREN. What?!

DANNY MA. Cool.

SHRIMP BOY. Chinese gotta stick together. Plus, we all look same!

(*Downstairs, pounding at the door. The sound of sirens, searchlights flood the room.*)

Here we go! You run! Me and Seven Girls, we hold 'em off!

DANNY MA. What? Me? No.

SHRIMP BOY. Can you handle that!

DANNY MA. I was just here for my phone!

(*An* **FBI AGENT** *busts into the room.*)

FBI AGENT. Freeze! FBI!

(**SHRIMP BOY** *pulls* **DANNY MA** *in front of him as cover, shoots.*)

DANNY MA. Wait wait wait wait –!

(*The* **FBI AGENT** *shoots* **DANNY MA** *in the head by accident.*)

LAUREN. Omigod, you killed him!

SHRIMP BOY. You kill the youth!

FBI AGENT. You're both coming with me.

LAUREN. I can't. I need to find my dad.

FBI AGENT. (*To walkie-talkie.*) I need backup.

SHRIMP BOY. You gotta get outta here.

FBI AGENT. Don't move!

SHRIMP BOY. We cover you.

LAUREN. Thank you!

SHRIMP BOY. And when you find you your dad back, you tell 'em all about the famous shrimp! You tell 'em his story! *Zao ah zao ah, naw wai gaw zi!**

LAUREN. I don't know what that means! I don't speak Chinese!

FBI AGENT. Me neither.

SHRIMP BOY. Go now!

> (*The* **FBI AGENT** *and* **SHRIMP BOY** *have a shootout as* **LAUREN** *leaps onto the balcony and then out the window.*)

LAUREN. Aaaaaah!

---

*Go now, I'll take care of it!

Chiropractor's Shop

(**LAUREN** *tumbles down into the darkness and hits something hard. When she wakes up, she is somewhere else. The blind* **CHIROPRACTOR** *faces her.*)

LAUREN. Where am I?

CHIROPRACTOR. You've had quite a fall.

LAUREN. Who are you?

CHIROPRACTOR. I'm the chiropractor. Welcome to my shop. The FBI came looking for you. Don't worry, I didn't rat you out. Said, "I haven't seen anyone like that lately." Which is true!

LAUREN. Why'd you help me?

CHIROPRACTOR. You're Larry's daughter. He got my son a job at the fortune cookie factory.

LAUREN. You're *my dad's* chiropractor! Your daughter works at American.

CHIROPRACTOR. You watch our back, we'll scratch yours!

LAUREN. You're the weird beard.

CHIROPRACTOR. You gotta have a gimmick! It helps with the tourists.

LAUREN. Well, thank you, but I have to get out of here –

(*The* **CHIROPRACTOR** *takes her pulse.*)

CHIROPRACTOR. – And find your father before it's too late?

LAUREN. Yes. How did you know?

CHIROPRACTOR. I can feel it in your pulse.

LAUREN. That's ridiculous.

CHIROPRACTOR. Chinese medicine. Sit down, relax. And I'll help you get you on your way.

LAUREN. But I have to – (*Clutches jaw.*) Aaaah.

CHIROPRACTOR. Careful! Talk too much you'll hurt yourself.

LAUREN. What did you do to me?

CHIROPRACTOR. Me? I fixed you. You're lucky you're speaking any Chinese at all.

LAUREN. Chinese? I don't speak Chinese.

CHIROPRACTOR. You sure? We're speaking it right now.

LAUREN. I've never known Chinese.

CHIROPRACTOR. But you're Chinese?

LAUREN. Yes?

CHIROPRACTOR. And your father's Chinese?

LAUREN. Yes?

CHIROPRACTOR. And your mother's Chinese?

LAUREN. Yes?

CHIROPRACTOR. And thousands and thousands of years back, all Chinese?

LAUREN. I guess?

CHIROPRACTOR. Then you're Chinese through and through. It's in your blood, your bones.

LAUREN. But I never learned how.

CHIROPRACTOR. Does a bird need to learn how to fly?

LAUREN. I don't know, I'm not a bird –

> *(The* **CHIROPRACTOR** *squeezes* **LAUREN***'s shoulder.)*

Aaaah!

CHIROPRACTOR. Feel that?

LAUREN. Yes, there! Ow!

CHIROPRACTOR. That bone? That is your Chinese. It's been out of alignment for years. I popped it back into place for you.

> *(***LAUREN*** massages her shoulder.)*

LAUREN. Aaah.

CHIROPRACTOR. Careful! The connection's not so great.

LAUREN. *(Re: shoulder.)* This is my Chinese?

CHIROPRACTOR. It's been there since the day you were born.

> *(The **CHIROPRACTOR** takes out a needle, aims it at **LAUREN**.)*

CHIROPRACTOR. Now let's get down to business!

LAUREN. What're you doing?

CHIROPRACTOR. I'm just gonna open up your third eye –

LAUREN. Wait wait wait wait / are you actually licensed to do this –?

CHIROPRACTOR. – Which is...approximately...right... around...there!

> *(The **CHIROPRACTOR** stabs the needle somewhere on **LAUREN**.)*

LAUREN. Aaah! I thought you were a chiropractor.

CHIROPRACTIC. Chiropractic acupuncturist.

LAUREN. Really?

CHIROPRACTIC ACUPUNCTURIST. Chinese medicine is holistic. We do everything. Now let me get your fourth eye.

LAUREN. Oh, I don't believe in that kind of –

> *(The **CHIROPRACTIC ACUPUNCTURIST** stabs the second needle in **LAUREN**. A fourth eye opens up.)*

Oh my god, that feels amazing.

> *(The **CHIROPRACTIC ACUPUNCTURIST** wiggles the needles in **LAUREN** like two joysticks. Different parts of her body react. Arms flail out, strange sounds, etc. Then **LAUREN** sees an image of her father.)*

Daddy?!

CHIROPRACTIC ACUPUNCTURIST. There he is!

> *(The **CHIROPRACTIC ACUPUNCTURIST** zooms in on **LARRY**, who is standing somewhere at a great height.)*

LAUREN. Where is he?

CHIROPRACTIC ACUPUNCTURIST. Somewhere on the other side of those doors.

LAUREN. Which doors? The Yee doors?

CHIROPRACTIC ACUPUNCTURIST. Those would be the ones.

LAUREN. Daddy! Daddy!

CHIROPRACTIC ACUPUNCTURIST. He can't hear you.

LAUREN. What is he doing?

CHIROPRACTIC ACUPUNCTURIST. He's looking for his name.

LAUREN. I don't understand.

(**LARRY** *seems to fall.*)

Daddy!

(*The reception goes out. The vision of* **LARRY** *fades.*)

CHIROPRACTIC ACUPUNCTURIST. Lost him.

LAUREN. How do I get him back?

CHIROPRACTIC ACUPUNCTURIST. You'll have to go through the doors first.

LAUREN. But the Yee doors don't open for me. I tried.

CHIROPRACTIC ACUPUNCTURIST. Some doors can't be opened on your own. Some doors gotta be opened for you.

LAUREN. By who?

CHIROPRACTIC ACUPUNCTURIST. The ancestors.

LAUREN. How do I get them to do that?

CHIROPRACTIC ACUPUNCTURIST. You must convince them you are worthy.

LAUREN. How?

CHIROPRACTIC ACUPUNCTURIST HERBALIST. I'm only a chiropractic acupunctural herbalist. If you're looking for answers, I'd consult the oracle.

LAUREN. Where do I find the oracle?

CHIROPRACTIC ACUPUNCTURIST HERBALIST. Portsmouth Square. Follow the cookies!

LAUREN. Cookies? What cookies?

CHIROPRACTIC ACUPUNCTURAL HERBALIST. Fortune cookies!

LAUREN. But I don't even know what the oracle looks like.

CHIROPRACTIC ACUPUNCTURAL HERBALIST. Go before it's –
   *tai ci.**

LAUREN. What did you say?

CHIROPRACTIC ACUPUNCTURAL HERBALIST. There it goes!
   The connection! It's – *mo jo la.***

> *(The spell is broken. The* **CHIROPRACTIC**
> **ACUPUNCTURAL HERBALIST** *can't speak any
> more English. He hardens into a stranger.)*

LAUREN. Wait, what happened to my Chinese?!

> *(**LAUREN** tries to adjust her shoulder back
> into place. Nothing.)*

CHIROPRACTIC ACUPUNCTURAL HERBALIST. *(Broken English.)*
   Okay. You find. This way.

LAUREN. But what were you saying?

CHIROPRACTIC ACUPUNCTURAL HERBALIST. Sorry. No English.

> *(The* **CHIROPRACTIC ACUPUNCTURAL HERBALIST**
> *has lost his magic, feels blindly around his
> shop.)*

LAUREN. But I'm not ready, I don't even know which way
   to –

> *(The* **CHIROPRACTOR** *is gone.)*

What am I supoosed to do now?

> *(**LAUREN***'s shoulder seems to tremble, pull her
> in a very specific direction.)*

Whoa! My Chinese!

> *(**LAUREN** follows its pull, exits.)*

---

*too late
**gone, you've lost it.

Hallway

ACTOR 1. Do you remember your mom?

ACTOR 2. I saw my mom this morning.

ACTOR 1. Sorry. *(Clarifies.)* Your birth mom.

ACTOR 2. Nah. I got adopted after she died, when I was really little.

ACTOR 1. *(Sympathetic.)* Aww.

ACTOR 2. I do have one memory of her.

ACTOR 1. Yeah?

ACTOR 2. This was back in Korea. She's singing to me. She's singing a song like –

> (**ACTOR 2** *hums an improvised, indistinct melody. We can't quite place it.*)

ACTOR 1. That's beautiful.

ACTOR 2. Then she kisses me on the forehead and says, "No one can stop what I must do. I swear I'll give my life for you." And then she goes behind a curtain and shoots herself.

ACTOR 1. Oh my god.

ACTOR 2. She gave up everything for me.

ACTOR 1. [Actor 2], I am so sorry.

ACTOR 2. Then my father comes in with his new wife, this white American woman. They see what's happened and take me home on the last helicopter out of the city instead of leaving me in Vietnam with the Engineer.

> *(Pause.)*

ACTOR 1. That's *Miss Saigon*.

ACTOR 2. What?

ACTOR 1. What you were describing was *Miss Saigon*. The musical.

ACTOR 2. No, I definitely remember my mom singing –

> (**ACTOR 2** *sings line from her mother's song again: "No one can stop what I must do. I swear I'll give my life for you." We now*

*recognize it as "I'd Give My Life For You"
from* Miss Saigon.)

ACTOR 1. Yeah, that's *Miss Saigon.*

ACTOR 2. Omigod. Do you know what this means?

ACTOR 1. Your parents once took you to see *Miss Saigon.*

ACTOR 2. No! It means I don't know where I come from.
And if I don't know where I come from, then it's like it
never happened! And I never was adopted and I never
grew up and I never went to Carnegie Mellon and I
never became an actor and so I never really existed!

ACTOR 1. Well, in marketing –

ACTOR 2. In marketing?

ACTOR 1. In marketing, when they're doing marketing
for different races, like black people marketing and
Hispanic people marketing, they just put the Asians in
with the whites.

ACTOR 2. What?!

ACTOR 1. Like our preferences are so closely aligned with
white people that we don't even count. To them, it's like
we don't even exist.

ACTOR 2. "We don't even exist."

(**ACTOR 2** *contemplates this.*)

Maybe that's why.

ACTOR 1. Why what?

ACTOR 2. Why she hasn't come back for us. Because "we
don't even exist."

ACTOR 1. That's ridiculous.

ACTOR 2. It's been forever. We can't possibly be on break
anymore.

ACTOR 1. If you're so worried, just check.

ACTOR 2. Maybe I will.

ACTOR 1. Good.

ACTOR 2. Where'd the door go?

ACTOR 1. It's right…there.

(Beat.)

Where's the door?!

(They look around. No door.)

Someone should call Equity.

(They begin to disappear.)

ACTOR 2. Oh shoot.

*(The **ACTORS** disappear from the scene.)*

ACTOR 1. Yep, there we go.

ACTOR 2. I left my charger in there.

*(The **ACTORS** are gone.)*

Portsmouth Square

(**LAUREN** *is dragged into the theater by her Chinese. It stops working.*)

LAUREN. "Follow the fortune cookies"? What fortune cookies?

(*A cookie drops into her hands from the sky.*)

You've got to be kidding me.

(*A flood of cookies continues to fall. She follows them through the audience.*)

Excuse me –

Sorry –

I just need to –

Ohp –

No, don't eat that please –

(*A large bag of cookies appears onstage.*)

Fortune cookies!

(*She arrives in Portsmouth Square on the stage.*)

Portsmouth Square. But where's the oracle?

(**LAUREN** *cracks open a fortune cookie. The ghostly* **LUM ELDERS** *appear.*)

LUM ELDERS. (**ACTORS 1, 2 & 3** *taking alternate lines.*) Aaaah.

Fortune cookies.

My favorite.

(*They feast on them.*)

LAUREN. Um, excuse me?

LUM ELDERS. Yes?

Yes?

Yes?

LAUREN. Someone said you might be able to help me?

LUM ELDERS. Help you?

Help how?

Now why would we want to do that?

LAUREN. Because...you're helpful ghosts?

LUM ELDERS. Hah.

Ho.

No.

(All.) Ghosts?

LAUREN. You're not ghosts...?

LUM ELDERS. Practically.

Nearly.

But no.

We're not.

Though we've been here so long we might as well be.

LAUREN. Then who are you?

LUM ELDERS. We run this place.

This place called Chinatown.

We are the Lum Elders.

LAUREN. Oh! The Lum Elders! My dad told me about you.

My dad. Larry Yee.

LUM ELDERS. Larry Yee?

No, Larry Yee.

No, Larry Yee.

Which one is it?

LAUREN. Uh, Larry...Yee.

LUM ELDERS. You mean Larry Yee.

Oh! Larry Yee.

(To **LAUREN**.*)* I thought you said Larry Yee.

Or Larry. Yee.

Chinese, it's a tonal language.

LAUREN. Anyway, my dad, I'm trying to find him. He's on the other side of the doors and I need to –

LUM ELDERS. Call to the ancestors to open the doors?

LAUREN. Yes!

LUM ELDERS. Well, the ancestors are Chinese ancestors.

And the doors are Chinese doors.

Which means –

(All.) A *bai*!

LAUREN. A what?

LUM ELDERS. A ritual.

A "hello, how are you and here's some stuff,"

To prove that you are worthy.

LAUREN. So how do I do a bai?

LUM ELDERS. *(All.)* Well, what do you have for us?

LAUREN. What're you talking about? I brought you cookies!

LUM ELDERS. And what else?

LAUREN. What else do you want?

LUM ELDERS. Nothing!

LAUREN. Nothing?

LUM ELDERS. So give us what we want!

LAUREN. But I can't give you something if there's nothing you want!

LUM ELDERS. We want nothing for ourselves.

Not "nothing for ourselves."

LAUREN. *(Realizes.)* That's right!

You don't want anything.

It's your grandkids that you care about!

LUM ELDERS. Go on.

LAUREN. Help me find my dad and I can help your grandkids with college applications.

LUM ELDERS. Can you?

LAUREN. I went to Yale. I can get them into wherever they want to go.

LUM ELDERS. A UC!

LAUREN. The University of California system, that's a start.

LUM ELDERS. Berkeley!

Davis!

Santa Cruz.

LAUREN. Great!

LUM ELDERS. San Diego! Riverside!

Irvine!

That's the Asian one.

LAUREN. Well, they're kind of all the Asian one.

LUM ELDERS. UCLA!

Santa Barbara.

Merced!

No, not that one.

Oh.

LAUREN. But if they go to Lowell, they must be able to get into a better school than / UCLA –

LUM ELDERS. A UC!

LAUREN. You want your grandkids to go to UCLA over Yale?

LUM ELDERS. Yes.

Go Bruins.

LAUREN. That makes absolutely no sense.

LUM ELDERS. You leave California

You go East Coast

And you never come back again.

LAUREN. That's not true. People come back.

LUM ELDERS. Did you?

LAUREN. I visit.

LUM ELDERS. You only come home for birthdays, weddings, and funerals.

LAUREN. Was I not supposed to live my life?

LUM ELDERS. A UC!

LAUREN. Fine, fine: a UC! Help me find my father and I'll help them get into a UC.

(The **LUM ELDERS** *confer for a moment, then:)*

LUM ELDERS. Three questions you will have.

No more.

No less.

Just three.

LAUREN. So how do I do a bai?

LUM ELDERS. To do the bai,
>   To honor the ancestors,
>   You must offer them the best of Chinatown.

LAUREN. Such as...?

LUM ELDERS. Well, let's see!

>   *(Out of the crumbs, the* **LUM ELDERS** *each pull out a perfectly intact fortune cookie, crack them open, and read the fortunes.)*

"Nothing loosens the tongue better than a little bit of drink."
In bed!
"The sweetest treat is the one you eat."
In bed!

LAUREN. This can't have anything to do with my father.

>   *(The* **LUM ELDERS** *gesture "patience.")*

LUM ELDERS. "Sometimes to get what you want, you have to be loud."

LUM ELDERS & LAUREN. In bed.

LUM ELDERS. Hey, that one's pretty good.

LAUREN. What does this all mean?

LUM ELDERS. *(Re: fortunes.)* This is your bai.
>   Your list from the ancestors.
>   The strongest whiskey,
>   The sweetest oranges,
>   The loudest firecrackers,
>   And all of it before sunset.

LAUREN. All that?

LUM ELDERS. And all for free.

LAUREN. Free? I can't possibly get all these things without money.

LUM ELDERS. Of course you can!
>   You're Larry's daughter.
>   Didn't he teach you the magic words?

LAUREN. No.

LUM ELDERS. Maybe he has
And maybe
You just haven't heard him.

LAUREN. I think I would've heard.

LUM ELDERS. There is hearing something
And there is hearing something.

LAUREN. What?

LUM ELDERS. *(Tries again.)* There is hearing something
And there is hearing something.

> *(The difference is too small for* **LAUREN** *or the audience to detect.)*

LAUREN. I still don't hear the difference.

LUM ELDERS. Of course you don't.

LAUREN. But what if I fail?

LUM ELDERS. If you don't find your father?

LAUREN. Yes.

LUM ELDERS. Nothing.

LAUREN. Nothing?

LUM ELDERS. He will return home
He will resume his normal life
But he will never be the same again.

LAUREN. You're lying.

LUM ELDERS. We see all.

LAUREN. Then show me.

LUM ELDERS. Beware!
Be careful!
You might not like what you see!

> *(The* **LUM ELDERS** *provide* **LAUREN** *with a vision: a future phone call between* **LARRY** *and* **LAUREN***.)*

FUTURE LARRY. Hello?

FUTURE LAUREN. Daddy.

FUTURE LARRY. Who is this?

FUTURE LAUREN. Lauren. It's Lauren.

FUTURE LARRY. Hello.

FUTURE LAUREN. How're you doing?

FUTURE LARRY. Nothing.

FUTURE LAUREN. No, I said "how." "How" are you doing?

FUTURE LARRY. I'm fine.

FUTURE LAUREN. You vote?

FUTURE LARRY. Hm?

FUTURE LAUREN. Election Day.

FUTURE LARRY. Oh. Guess I forgot.

FUTURE LAUREN. Get Mom to take you.

FUTURE LARRY. That's okay.

FUTURE LAUREN. "You gotta vote! For the Chinese community!"

FUTURE LARRY. Uh-huh.

FUTURE LAUREN. "You don't vote, who knows what could happen!"

FUTURE LARRY. Okay. I gotta go.

FUTURE LAUREN. I met a Yee over the weekend. He lives in Munich. We had lunch. So two! Two German Yees. Ah ah ah.

FUTURE LARRY. My TV program's starting.

FUTURE LAUREN. When can I come visit?

FUTURE LARRY. *(Bad connection, can't hear.)* What?

FUTURE LAUREN. I want to come visit.

FUTURE LARRY. *(Still can't hear.)* Okay, it's starting. I'll tell Mom you called. Thank you for calling.

FUTURE LAUREN. I love you.

FUTURE LARRY. Bye bye.

> *(The vision fades out.)*

LAUREN. That's not my father.

LUM ELDERS. Not the father you know.
Not the father you knew.
But if you don't find him
Before sunset

Your father will become a wall to you
Like you never knew him at all.
And in your children
– If you have them –
There will remain a hole inside of them
Shaped like a door
Never to be entered.
(All.) Or are we not the Lum Elders who know all?

> *(The* **LUM ELDERS** *begin to drift away.)*

LAUREN. Where are you going?!

LUM ELDERS. Three questions you had
And three questions you asked!

> *(The* **LUM ELDERS** *smell something new.)*

LAUREN. Wait wait wait! I still need your help!

LUM ELDERS. *(All.)* I smell cookies...

> *(The* **LUM ELDERS** *disappear.)*

LAUREN. The strongest whiskey,
The sweetest oranges,
The loudest firecrackers,
All before sunset and all for free.

A Wine and Spirits Store

LAUREN. Wait, I know this!
Left on Washington, right on Grant.
The store with the red awning!

>(**LAUREN** *sees the liquor store.*)

This is the place my dad told me about!

>(**LAUREN** *enters. Jingle of a bell. The* **WHISKEY SELLER** *appears. She is very smiley, friendly. Her accent is almost Midwestern.*)

WHISKEY SELLER. Hi, there!

LAUREN. Hello.

WHISKEY SELLER. Just to let you know, we're closing soon, so you let me know if there's anything we can help you with.

LAUREN. ...This is a store.

WHISKEY SELLER. Yep!

LAUREN. Where I can just ask you for something?

WHISKEY SELLER. You betcha.

LAUREN. Oh, thank god! I need some whiskey. I need "the strongest whiskey in Chinatown."

WHISKEY SELLER. Then this'll be the one.

>(*The* **WHISKEY SELLER** *whips out a beautiful bottle of whiskey, pours* **LAUREN** *a sample.*)

Goes down smooth, doesn't it? So you'll take this one? I can pack it up, gift-wrap it, you tell me. (*Stops.*) Everything okay?

LAUREN. This can't be the strongest whiskey in Chinatown.

WHISKEY SELLER. Oh no?

LAUREN. The label's in English.

WHISKEY SELLER. Is it?

LAUREN. It says it was made in Wisconsin.

WHISKEY SELLER. That's a typo.

LAUREN. I don't want this tourist shit.

WHISKEY SELLER. Pardon?

LAUREN. Give me the good cheap stuff.

> (*The* **WHISKEY SELLER** *looks more closely at* **LAUREN**.)

WHISKEY SELLER. Ohhh. You mean something a little more like this?

> (*The* **WHISKEY SELLER** *uncorks an ancient whiskey jug.* **LAUREN** *smells, gags.*)

LAUREN. Yes! That! I want that.

WHISKEY SELLER. You betcha. But first, cash? Credit?

> (**LAUREN** *starts for her wallet, then:*)

LAUREN. I can't pay you.

WHISKEY SELLER. Excuse me?

LAUREN. I'm doing a bai –

WHISKEY SELLER. A what?

LAUREN. A ritual. And if I want it to work, I can't give you any money.

> (*The* **WHISKEY SELLER**'s *tourist-friendly veneer dissipates, the Chinatown in her begins to come out. Maybe she starts chain-smoking, spitting in the middle of the store.*)

WHISKEY SELLER. Then why would I give it to you?

LAUREN. Um, because I'm Larry Yee's daughter? And sometimes you give him things for free?

WHISKEY SELLER. I don't know him, I don't know you, and all you American-born have money. I know it. I can smell the money on you.

LAUREN. Yes, but right now, I can't. So do me this one favor and –

WHISKEY SELLER. Sorry. I got four kids to feed.

LAUREN. I got a father to find.

WHISKEY SELLER. I could be deported at any moment.

LAUREN. I only have till sunset.

WHISKEY SELLER. I got Hep B and no health insurance.

LAUREN. I got the FBI on my tail.

WHISKEY SELLER. I'm FOB and I sell my tail.

LAUREN. I only come home for birthdays, weddings, and funerals.

WHISKEY SELLER. I don't know what a birthday is because I've never had one.

LAUREN. I never rest.

WHISKEY SELLER. I never sleep.

LAUREN. I never eat.

WHISKEY SELLER. I never breathe.

LAUREN. That's impossible.

WHISKEY SELLER. I just wait in a semi-catatonic state, seven days a week, eighteen hours a day for less than minimum wage, until someone comes along and demands I give them my things for free. Like I don't got four kids to worry about.

LAUREN. I may never have them.

WHISKEY SELLER. I never leave this place.

LAUREN. I never come here if I don't have to.

WHISKEY SELLER. Not even to sleep.

LAUREN. Not even to see my grandparents.

WHISKEY SELLER. My kids, they never see me.

LAUREN. We never spoke.

WHISKEY SELLER. We never talk.

LAUREN. Because they only knew Chinese. Because I would rather not do something than do it incorrectly.

WHISKEY SELLER. I don't even think they remember my name.

LAUREN. And sometimes I think Chinatown is a filthy broken ghetto that should just be erased.

WHISKEY SELLER. One day I hope it will.

LAUREN. You do?

WHISKEY SELLER. – Haggle with me –

LAUREN. What?

WHISKEY SELLER. – Haggle with me –

LAUREN. Oh, um, I don't really know how to haggle, but um, it's not that good.

WHISKEY SELLER. It's the best!

LAUREN. ...No, it's not.

WHISKEY SELLER. Imported. Made of one hundred percent pure ingredients.

LAUREN. Are you kidding me? I see them selling this across the street, cheaper, half price, new bottle. Not like this old stuff. You should be paying me to take it off your hands.

WHISKEY SELLER. Twenty dollars.

LAUREN. How about free?

WHISKEY SELLER. How about ten?

LAUREN. How about free?

WHISKEY SELLER. How about five?

LAUREN. How about free?

> *(The* **WHISKEY SELLER** *hands her the ancient whiskey jug.)*

WHISKEY SELLER. You are his daughter. And you are worthy.

LAUREN. Thank you.

WHISKEY SELLER. And when you find you your father back, tell Larry he needs to come by, fix our phones. They don't work.

LAUREN. I will.

> *(A* **LION DANCE** *sneaks by with a bag full of oranges.)*

What is he holding?

WHISKEY SELLER. Looks like the sweetest oranges in Chinatown.

> *(The* **LION DANCE** *bounds onstage with the oranges.)*

LAUREN. My oranges!

> *(The* **LION DANCE** *runs off.)*

LAUREN. Lion dance! Wait, lion dance!

(**LAUREN** *runs off after the* **LION DANCE.**)

Chinese Playground

(**LAUREN** *hurries after the* **LION DANCE**.)

LAUREN. Hey, boy. Hey, boy. I'm not gonna hurt you, I just need to –

(*The* **LION DANCE** *begins to eat the bag of oranges.*)

Oh wait wait wait wait –

(*The* **LION DANCE** *has eaten the bag of oranges.*)

Oh no no no.

(*Then she realizes –*)

Wait, you didn't eat that. Just like my dad said. You pretend to eat it and then you spit it back out. So – spit it back out.

(**LAUREN** *waits. The* **LION DANCE** *shrugs.*)

Come on, please! It's almost sunset. What do I have to do to get the oranges back?

(*The* **LION DANCE** *gestures "hit it!" The sound of lion dance music, clanging cymbals, drums.* The **LION DANCE** *sways to the music, gestures for* **LAUREN** *to follow it.*)

No.

LION DANCE. ("No?")

LAUREN. I don't dance.

LION DANCE. ("Everyone can dance.")

LAUREN. I never learned. All the lessons were in Chinese!

(*The* **LION DANCE** *starts to leave.*)

Wait wait wait don't go! Okay. Okay? Look, I'm doing it. I'm doing it.

---

*A license to produce *King of the Yees* does not include a performance license for any third-party or copyrighted music. Licensees should create an original composition or use music in the public domain. For further information, please see Music Use Note on page 3.

(LAUREN does a move.)

LAUREN. See?

(LAUREN learns to sync up with the LION DANCE's moves.)

This is kind of fun.

(The LION DANCE and LAUREN perform a dance together. Finally, the LION DANCE spits back out the bag of oranges.)

Got it! Thank you! Now all I need are the firecrackers.

(The LION DANCE gestures.)

You know where the firecrackers are?

(The LION DANCE nods.)

Over by the alley? Which alley?

(The LION DANCE takes off. LAUREN follows.)

An Alley

(**LAUREN** *runs down a dark alley, lost. The* **LION DANCE** *is nowhere to be seen.*)

LAUREN. Lion dance?

(*The street lamps flicker on.*)

Lion dance?

(*The* **SICHUAN FACE CHANGER** *appears.*)

SICHUAN FACE CHANGER. Need some help?

LAUREN. Who're you?

SICHUAN FACE CHANGER. Don't you know?

(*A different face is put on.*)

Can't you tell?

(*A different face is put on.*)

Isn't it as plain as the face on my face?

LAUREN. You're the Sichuan face changer!

SICHUAN FACE CHANGER. That's right!

LAUREN. What're you doing here?

SICHUAN FACE CHANGER. I heard you were doing a bai, that you needed some help. So here I am.

LAUREN. I need the loudest firecrackers in Chinatown.

(*The* **SICHUAN FACE CHANGER** *takes out an unassuming box of firecrackers.*)

SICHUAN FACE CHANGER. Here you go.

(*Before* **LAUREN** *can grab the firecrackers, he closes his fist on them.*)

But the price is one riddle.

LAUREN. That's it?

SICHUAN FACE CHANGER. That's all.

LAUREN. Thank you.

SICHUAN FACE CHANGER. But if you fail, I take your face.

LAUREN. My what?

SICHUAN FACE CHANGER. Answer wrong and your face is mine.

LAUREN. This face?

SICHUAN FACE CHANGER. Make your choice. It's almost sunset.

LAUREN. Who are you?

SICHUAN FACE CHANGER. Maybe I'm a friend.

>   *(A different face is put on.)*

Or maybe I'm not.

Maybe I'm the playwright

Who writes about places she doesn't know

People she doesn't understand

And doors that won't open for her.

>   *(He puts on his Larry face.)*

Or maybe I'm just a telephone man.

>   *(For a brief moment,* **LAUREN** *sees* **LARRY** *flash by.)*

LAUREN. Daddy!

SICHUAN FACE CHANGER. Whose story you will never know Whose true face you will never see.

LAUREN. You're lying!

SICHUAN FACE CHANGER. But the more you say it!

LAUREN. Then tell me the riddle because I am going to find my father!

SICHUAN FACE CHANGER. And if you fail?

LAUREN. You get my face.

SICHUAN FACE CHANGER. Splendid.

>   *(The riddle.)*

"I am rich but poor, bitter but sweet.

I am hard to know, but easy to meet.

I've been a jailor, a protector, a stranger, a friend.

A lie, an illusion, a means to an end.

I shrink and I die in all but few cases,

Yet, seem to grow in the most unusual places.
And if you are lucky, if you scale that wall,
Then one day your children will not know me at all."

> *(Beat.)*

LAUREN. *(Small.)* I don't know.

SICHUAN FACE CHANGER. What was that?

LAUREN. Nothing could be that many things at once.

SICHUAN FACE CHANGER. That's where you're wrong.

> *(The sun begins to set.)*

LAUREN. Please! You have to give me more time!

SICHUAN FACE CHANGER. You Yees always think you have more time.

> *(The **SICHUAN FACE CHANGER** reveals a knife and begins to close in on **LAUREN**.)*

One face, please.

LAUREN. No, no, no, you can't! I have to find my dad! I've been running around all day, I've been going all around – *(Stops.)* Chinatown.

SICHUAN FACE CHANGER. What?

LAUREN. "I am rich but poor, bitter but sweet.
I am hard to know, but easy to meet.
And if you are lucky, if you scale that wall,
Then one day your children will not know me at all."

> *(Beat.)*

The answer is Chinatown.

> *(Pause.)*

I'm right. I know I'm right.

> *(The **SICHUAN FACE CHANGER** rips off his last mask. We see his true face.)*

SICHUAN FACE CHANGER. That is correct.

> *(He gives her the firecrackers.)*

LAUREN. Thank you!

SICHUAN FACE CHANGER. Who do you think you are?

LAUREN. You know who I am? I'm Larry Yee's daughter. And I'm the one who's getting my father back.

(**LAUREN** *hurries off. A bell begins to toll.*)

SICHUAN FACE CHANGER. Hurry! You wouldn't want to miss that sunset!

Yee Fung Toy

(**LAUREN** *runs back to the Yee Fung Toy headquarters with her bundle of ingredients. She stands at the red double doors, waits. Nothing happens.*)

LAUREN. I've got it! I've got the bai.

The strongest whiskey

The sweetest oranges

The loudest firecrackers

And all of it before sunset!

(*The sun continues to set.*)

C'mon!

What am I doing wrong? How am I not worthy?

(**LAUREN** *takes a step back, thinks.*)

"I am Lauren Yee! Open these doors!"

(*Nothing.*)

I command you! I am commanding you.

(*Beat.*)

Don't ignore me! I know you can hear me! If you can hear me, then – (*Realizes.*) Chinese doors. You're Chinese doors.

(**LAUREN** *snaps her own shoulder back into place.*)

Ow, that – *ho tong ah!*[*]

(*The wall seems to respond.*)

Hoi mun![**]

(*The wall seems to respond.*)

---

[*]hurts so much
[**]Door.

LAUREN. *Naw hai Yee siu gook. Hoi mun. Nay hai yu gah gei mun hoi mun ah. Hoy mun ah!**

    (The doors open.)

*M goy!***

    *(**LAUREN** leaps through the doors.)*

---

*I am Lauren Yee. Open these doors. You are the Yee family doors. You open for me. Now.
**Thank you!

The Other Side of the Doors

> (**LAUREN** *lands somewhere, hard.*)

LAUREN. Daddy?!
I'm here.
I'm here for you!
Daddy?

> (*An explosion of firecrackers and a poof of smoke. Out of the smoke, a hand appears.*)

What the –

> (*The hand snaps, extends into the* **MODEL ANCESTOR**, *the living embodiment of the portrait hanging in every Yee Family Association branch. Possibly channels the energy of RuPaul.*)

MODEL ANCESTOR. Oooh, I hear descendants!

LAUREN. Model Ancestor?!

MODEL ANCESTOR. Thass right. Welcome to the other side.

LAUREN. I thought you were just a story.

MODEL ANCESTOR. Girl, where you think you come from, if there is no Model Ancestor?

LAUREN. I guess.

MODEL ANCESTOR. Okay, okay, let's see what you brought your Model Ancestor –

> (*The* **MODEL ANCESTOR** *puts on his glasses, looks at* **LAUREN**.)

Aw hell no.

LAUREN. What?

MODEL ANCESTOR. Girrrrl, you can't be here. This place is for Yees only.

LAUREN. I am a Yee.

MODEL ANCESTOR. (*Reaches a hand out, feels her aura.*) Yeah, you ain't a Yee. You some kind of cylinder.

LAUREN. Zwillinger.

MODEL ANCESTOR. Whatever. And we cannot be having that. So shoo. Shoo.

> (*The* **MODEL ANCESTOR** *shoos her away.*)

LAUREN. I did a bai. You opened your doors for me.

MODEL ANCESTOR. Now why would I do that?

LAUREN. Because I'm worthy. Because I've always been.

> (**LAUREN** *hands the* **MODEL ANCESTOR** *her bundle.*)

MODEL ANCESTOR. I see you got that Yee attitude, okay.

> (*The* **MODEL ANCESTOR** *grabs the whiskey out of the bundle.*)

Oooh, you got me that good cheap stuff!

LAUREN. It was free.

MODEL ANCESTOR. So my humble descendant, what can I do for you?

LAUREN. I'm looking for my dad.

MODEL ANCESTOR. Who?

LAUREN. Larry Yee?

MODEL ANCESTOR. Girl, do you see this place?

I got Yees up in my Yees.

Might as well be a fucking Wong convention.

You want a Larry Yee? You gotta be more specific than that.

LAUREN. Oh right. Larry Yee.

MODEL ANCESTOR. Oh, Larry Yee! You're his daughter! You the story Yee!

LAUREN. How do you know that?

MODEL ANCESTOR. He told me all about you. He just came by "trying to get his name back."

LAUREN. He did?

MODEL ANCESTOR. Yeah, they turn sixty and show up at your door, real chatty.

LAUREN. So where is he now?

MODEL ANCESTOR. He ain't here no more, baby.

LAUREN. I missed him?! But the Lum Elders told me I had till sunset!

MODEL ANCESTOR. Girl, the sun set hours ago.

LAUREN. I was late?!

MODEL ANCESTOR. You a Yee, we always late.

LAUREN. But I was told that if I did a bai, you'd open the doors, and I'd get my dad back.

MODEL ANCESTOR. Yeah, but before you get you your dad back, there's one more person you gotta face.

LAUREN. Who?!

MODEL ANCESTOR. Larry Yee.

LAUREN. My dad?

MODEL ANCESTOR. Girl, you gotta go back and talk to your dad, instead of talking to your dad. And I know you hear the difference.

LAUREN. I don't know if I can do that.

MODEL ANCESTOR. You aced every test just as good as Larry Yee, and you still don't know what you gonna say to your own dad?

LAUREN. Not what. How.

I don't know how to talk to him.

I never have.

What if I go back and I still don't know him? What if I never do?

MODEL ANCESTOR. That is always a possibility.

LAUREN. I don't like that.

MODEL ANCESTOR. 'Cause you would rather not do something than do it incorrect?

LAUREN. Yes.

MODEL ANCESTOR. Honey, you think I knew what I was doing when I fled to save y'all's asses from being slaughtered?

LAUREN. No?

MODEL ANCESTOR. No, I did not. And you think I wanted to walk to Southern China? In these heels?

LAUREN. No –

MODEL ANCESTOR. Hell to the no, I did not.

But I did what I had to.

And you can, too.

'Cause by my watch, you still got time.

> (**LAUREN** *still hesitates.*)

But you don't got forever.

> (**MODEL ANCESTOR** *offers* **LAUREN** *a sip of the whiskey. She takes a sip.*)

Girl, you about to throw down with your dad, you gonna need a bigger sip than that.

> (**LAUREN** *sips again, makes a face.*)

LAUREN. Ugh.

MODEL ANCESTOR. Yeah, you get what you pay for.

LAUREN. Goodbye, Model Ancestor.

MODEL ANCESTOR. Oh, I see you soon. Drop by when you turn sixty.

LAUREN. Model Ancestor, I'm not even close to sixty.

MODEL ANCESTOR. Girl, it will come faster than you think.

> (**MODEL ANCESTOR** *smoke bombs the stage and disappears.*)

Go Yees! And fuck those Wongs.

Yee Fung Toy

(**LARRY** *is taking down the remaining Leland Yee signs. It's morning.* **LAUREN** *enters the space. She watches him for a moment. He's on the phone.*)

LARRY. Hey, Dee.

Yeah, I'm at the association.

Yeah, I'll call the restaurant, try to get the deposit back.

I just gotta go by Nineteenth Avenue first.

(**LARRY** *hangs up. He stands there for a moment. He looks at the association's walls. Then he sees* **LAUREN**.)

Lauren.

LAUREN. I found you. I went all over Chinatown last night looking for you.

LARRY. I wasn't in Chinatown. Couldn't face 'em at the dinner.

LAUREN. I thought I'd lost you.

LARRY. I was taking down the signs instead.

LAUREN. You were getting your name back.

LARRY. Nearly broke my neck trying to get the ones up on Geary. Still gotta get the ones down on Nineteenth Avenue.

LAUREN. Sunset.

LARRY. Yeah.

LAUREN. You haven't hit the Sunset District.

LARRY. Last one left.

LAUREN. So it's still "before sunset." The Lum Elders were right. I wasn't late. I was on time.

LARRY. I gotta go get the rest.

LAUREN. Don't go. Not yet.

LARRY. I gotta! Before someone sees 'em.

LAUREN. Why?

LARRY. That is my name up there.

LAUREN. You're not Leland.

LARRY. But I'm his sign guy. His hatchet man. If there's a sign up there, it's because of me.

LAUREN. Then let me help you.

LARRY. Not your job.

LAUREN. I am your daughter, that is my job.

LARRY. We gotta get you to the airport, catch your flight. No time to help.

LAUREN. I have time.

> *(Beat.)*

I'm flying American.

LARRY. So?

LAUREN. I'll just call your chiropractor's daughter. I'll get her to change my flight. I'll tell her I'm Larry's daughter. I want to talk.

LARRY. About what?

LAUREN. About everything I don't know.

LARRY. So you can write it down. For your play.

LAUREN. So I can know.

LARRY. As long as I give you the dirt.

LAUREN. I don't want the dirt. I want you.

LARRY. Why?

LAUREN. Because I'm your daughter.

LARRY. And?

LAUREN. And a playwright.

LARRY. And?

LAUREN. I live in New York, but I'm moving to Berlin.

LARRY. Are you excited?

LAUREN. Yes.

LARRY. Are you nervous?

LAUREN. Yes.

LARRY. Why?

LAUREN. Because I am afraid. I am afraid I will leave and I will lose you and I will have loved someone that I never really knew.

LARRY. I'm just a telephone man.

LAUREN. And?

LARRY. And a member of the Yee Fung Toy.

LAUREN. And?

LARRY. And I never really thought I'd have kids.

LAUREN. Really?

LARRY. And I never thought I'd join the association.

LAUREN. Why did you?

LARRY. Because I'm a Yee.

LAUREN. And?

LARRY. And my dad was a member.

LAUREN. And?

LARRY. And when he died, I just felt naked.
Like I had no idea how I was supposed to go on.

LAUREN. How did you?

LARRY. You ready for that?

LAUREN. Yes.

LARRY. Well, when my dad turned sixty, he told me:
"Larry, there will come a time when I will not remember you
I will not remember that I love you
I will not remember that you are my son.
And so you gotta say it for me
So that even if I look at you and I do not remember any of this,
It will always remain true."
And so I said it
Every day
So that when the time came
I could still believe that deep down inside of him
There was a door

That would always be the very center of him.

I had to remember this so that he would not become a wall to me.

And one day you will need to say things for me because only then will it remain true.

LAUREN. You're right. I'm not ready for that.

LARRY. We never are.

> (**LARRY** *starts to continue on their journey.*
> **LAUREN** *takes a breath.*)

LAUREN. Well, "there was my dad –"

LARRY. *(Nods.)* "There was my dad –"

LAUREN. "Larry. Larry Yee."

LARRY. "And he was always on time."

LAUREN. "And he was always on time."

> (**LARRY** *gives his daughter the stage.*)

And right now we are in [name of theater, name of city] at the end of our play.

A play that I thought would be about the past.

About dying Chinatowns.

About how things fall apart and how to say goodbye.

But I was wrong.

That's not what I was writing.

The story I wrote, this play, is not about the end, but the beginning.

What we both have yet to discover.

I realize it's a little late in our story to start something new.

But plays take a long time to write and I always think I have more time.

I try so hard to get it right, but there is still so much I do not know.

But what I do know:

Today is [today's date].

The time is [the current time].

The temperature is [today's temperature].

I am a Yee.

And this is my story.

So that I will always know that deep down, yes, there is a door

And a way for me to enter.

End of Play

CPSIA information can be obtained
at www.ICGtesting.com
Printed in the USA
LVHW081935170821
695131LV00027B/236